Arnold E. Bender BSc, PhD, DSc (Hon, Madrid), FRSH, FIFST, recently retired as Professor of Nutrition and Dietetics at the University of London and as Head of the Department of Food Science and Nutrition at Queen Elizabeth College, London. A world authority on nutrition, Professor Bender is the author of several textbooks and a popular lecturer and broadcaster. He serves on a number of important Government committees and is Vice-President of the International Union of Food Science and Technology.

Professor Bender's main areas of research have been in protein nutrition, the effects of food processing on the nutritional value of foods, the nutritional aspects of legumes as human food and the nutrition of schoolchildren – resulting in about 150 published papers in various British and foreign scientific journals. He is frequently called upon to advise companies, consumer groups and others on matters relating to nutrition, health and foods.

D1428330

Health Or Hoax?

The truth behind health foods and diets

ARNOLD E. BENDER

SPHERE BOOKS LIMITED

First published in Great Britain by
Elvendon Press, 1985
Copyright © Arnold E. Bender, 1985
Introduction © Arnold E. Bender, 1986
Published by Sphere Books Ltd, 1986
27, Wright's Lane, London W8 5SW

TRADE
MARK

Set in Plantin

Printed and bound in Great Britain by
Collins, Glasgow

CONTENTS

INTRODUCTION
to Second Edition

Just what is a health food? The answer is that there is no such thing, but there is certainly a health food business – and it is big business. In Britain there are 1500 'health food' shops. Their turnover increased from £30 million in 1973 to £120 million in 1983 and is growing rapidly. Some 600 shops are banded together under the umbrella of Booker Health Foods, which also owns 180 Holland and Barrett shops plus 30 franchised outlets growing at the rate of 20 to 30 a year, 90 Kingswood pharmacies and Newman Turner Publications (as well as a 47.6% stake in the American manufacturing company P. Leiner). There is nothing necessarily wrong with such a large-scale operation, although frequent articles appear in health magazines reviling food from such sources.

The produce sold in these shops ranges from ordinary foods grown under conditions that are claimed (without any justification) to produce superior quality, and some relatively unusual foods, to pills, potions, herbal remedies, extracts of plants and of animal organs, and dietary supplements bewildering in their complexity and multiplicity. You can buy vitamin C as a loose powder, in tablets – chewable or not – as ascorbic acid, as sodium ascorbate, as a mixture of these two, as calcium ascorbate, as magnesium ascorbate, with or without flavonoids (see page 92), pure or 75% pure (!) with or without milk base, and mixed with any number of other vitamins that may or may not be claimed to enhance its effect. To guide you through this maze you can buy books and magazines or even obtain free news-sheets which extol the virtues of one product and denigrate its rivals.

Some of these products, such as RNA and DNA (page 60), single amino acids (page 88) and apricot kernels (page 81), are known to be harmful and others, such as pollen, bees' royal jelly and ginseng cigarettes (cigarettes in a health food shop!), have never been tested for safety. Most are probably harmless but are sold with extravagant and unsupported claims.

When *Health or Hoax?* was first published in hardback, I participated in some five hours of radio phone-in programmes. These did not arouse a single listener who wanted to defend these products. Indeed many said – and wrote – that it came like a breath of fresh air. However, the health food trade has its apologists, and one of their criticisms was that the book was based on much old material. Certainly, this was unavoidable, so let me add some new material. Cantamega 1000, currently on sale, is claimed to be 'fibre-rich' – it has 700 milligrams of fibre in the daily tablet compared with the average intake of 20 *grams*. Cantamega 2000 and Larkhall Laboratories Strong B Complex still contain apricot kernels despite the fact that this was banned from over-the-counter sales in 1984 (see page 82). In *Health Standard (Issue No. 3)* it was claimed that Larkhall Laboratories was 'the only company to fight to the finish' – and apparently beyond the finish – 'for its (laetrile's) availability'. Furthermore, despite the limit finally set on the amount of vitamin A in products by the Health Food Manufacturers Association after frequent complaints of vitamin A poisoning (see page 154), the same article boasted that 'Larkhall Laboratories is still fighting to preserve the availability of potent supplements'.

A recent leaflet for Pollen B claims that 'nutritionists state that man could live adequately on pollen alone'. That would require about 4000 tablets a day and would almost certainly prove fatal.

The story of E330 (see page 18) can be brought up to date. The hoax is now ten years old and has been thoroughly discredited yet it was revived and recirculated by a health food shop in the Isle of Wight (according to a correspondent who wrote in to the Thames Television programme 'What It's Worth', screened on 18 July 1985). Since the facts were well known at the time and had been published by the Ministry of Agriculture, the repetition of such deliberate falsehoods says little for the integrity of the promoters.

Untrue statements are still being made. Power Health Products claims that lysine is an essential amino acid, which means that the body cannot make it (true) and that a dietary supplement is essential for health (untrue – see page 89). Starch blockers have been shown to be useless (see page 177) but are still sold.

'Natural' is an in word used by almost everyone, especially in the health food literature and on labels. We can have natural bran, toasted natural bran and natural toasted bran, natural packaged tomato soup made from natural ingredients, natural wheat germ milled in the traditional way (surely traditional flour included the germ), even natural baked beans (using apple juice instead of natural sugar), naturally produced meat, natural sweets, natural biscuits, and, if you like, you can go on natural healing holidays and even buy a clothes conditioner with a natural smell (farmyard?).

The health food trade sums itself up in the magazine *Here's Health (May 1985. p. 6)*: 'The problem is that before being awarded a full licence every (natural) medicine is being reviewed by the Department of Health to check its safety, quality and efficacy.' That is a problem?

It is well worth remembering that the basis of the health food business, as indeed all businesses, is making a healthy profit. *Your Health*, a leaflet describing the Booker McConnell Group's investments in 'health products', states 'Our business – as suppliers and distributors – continues to offer exciting opportunities for profitable growth.' 'Holland and Barrett will continue to benefit from the growing interest in the nutritional aspects of health.' Indeed, the evidence that so-called health foods are profitable, apart from the prices, comes from the growing sales of these products in ordinary supermarkets and the fact that a third of chemists' shops have gone into the business. It is to explain the facts behind the claims made by this profitable industry that this book has been written.

Arnold E. Bender
August 1985

1

SCIENCE OR SALESMANSHIP?

WHAT ARE HEALTH FOODS?

There is no such thing as a health food. The term is both false and misleading – misleading because it suggests that other foods are unhealthy.

Certainly some foods contain more nutrients than others. Milk contains protein, fats and carbohydrates, and is rich in calcium and vitamins A and B2, with small amounts of other vitamins. Butter contains only fat, some vitamin A and a trace of vitamin D. Many of the traditional foods which we have eaten since biblical times – such as olives, honey and dates – are very poor sources of nutrients even when they are 'natural', that is, not even dried by the sun. Yet they are often promoted as 'health foods' because they are of ancient origin and are unprocessed. In fact, fresh dates are sixty-five per cent sugar. Honey is a mixture of two sugars, glucose and fructose, and apart from its pleasant flavour, has only small traces of any other nutrients. Fresh olives contain less than one per cent protein and most of the rest, apart from water, is fat (olive oil).

So we could certainly not live on these foods alone. As it happens, there is no single food, apart from human milk for babies, which supplies all the nutrients we need.

Attempts have been made from time to time to define 'health foods' but since the term itself is false, these definitions are all open to criticism. For example, one attempt defined them as 'whole foods', presumably meaning whole wheat as

1

compared with white flour or milled cereals. Would this then mean that unpeeled potatoes, apples and oranges could be called 'health foods', but that their peeled counterparts would not be eligible for this title of apparent distinction?

A similar problem occurred, as I will discuss later, when a legal definition was sought for 'organically' grown foods and 'natural' foods. Neither term is acceptable – they have no meaning and therefore cannot be defined.

This does not stop health food shops from making extravagant claims, however. Health food shops sell a variety of foods (some unusual, many the same as those available in supermarkets), food supplements and extracts, pills and potions. Some are useful, some are not very useful but are innocuous, and some are dangerous. When foods of various kinds are promoted as so-called health foods, far-ranging claims are made for them. It is these claims that are criticized by scientists. Few, if any, of the claims have ever been investigated, therefore making it impossible for their promoters to substantiate them.

Some health food products are promoted in all sincerity by people who may feel that they, personally, have benefited from them or who believe that unprocessed, 'natural' foods must be better than their commercially produced equivalents. The degree of sincerity ranges across the spectrum from the honest and sincere 'believer' to the cowboy and swindler who are just out to make a 'fast buck' at the expense of gullible passers-by. Some, indeed, have been taken to court and fined for breaking the law, revealing their innate dishonesty by immediately returning to the market place to sell another fake product until that in its turn is prohibited.

All this obviously makes it difficult for the man or woman in the street to know who is telling the truth. At the present time, when health food promoters freely turn any tentative research finding into hard, proven 'fact', one must almost have a degree in both nutrition and food science to be able to sort out the sheep from the goats. In the following pages I have attempted to do this, but we must still remember that the products themselves, and the claims made for them, can differ

2

enormously from one manufacturer or salesman to another. A modicum of reason and logic are necessary to help discount claims for foods, herbal remedies and unusual plant and animal extracts as cures for everything under the sun, plus the soul and spirit.

WHAT THE MANUFACTURERS SAY

The statement that there is no such thing as a health food is confirmed by attempts made to define them over a three-year period by the Health Food Manufacturers Association (UK) in conjunction with the European Federation of Associations of Health Food Manufacturers. The suggested definition consisted of a number of descriptions:

1 'Products primarily prepared with the specific intention of maintaining and/or improving health.' This would not include any 'natural' foods which are, of course, not grown or produced primarily for such purposes, e.g. whole grains, fruits and vegetables.

2 'They are as naturally based as possible.' Therefore apples, oranges, cabbage, watercress and everything grown, whether animal, vegetable, fish or fowl, could be called a health food.

3 'Such products should be provided with consumer information regarding their health benefits, therefore they are preferably sold in specialist stores by trained staff.' Judging from the wild, extravagant and often illegal claims made for so-called 'health foods' this is sheer impudence.

4 'Health foods include foods with their full nutritional content.' This would therefore take in unpeeled potatoes, fish with their viscera, olives but not olive oil and everything else that is sold (if not actually eaten) without the removal of any part.

5 'Food supplements selected to supply nutrients lacking in

the diet to prevent deficiency.' In view of the inaccurate claims made by many of the major health food manufacturers about supplements of no proven value such as the non-existent vitamins B13, B15, B17, lecithin, pollen, royal jelly, sesame seeds, carob beans, etc. etc. this is a very twisted piece of thinking.

6 'In addition to health products there may also be appropriate literature and equipment which assist the maintenance and development of good health.' Since much of the literature, at least, is the invention of copy writers it would have to be excluded from the definition.

The final section, section IV, includes 'the careful selection of high quality raw material – with a minimum of synthetic pesticides and other harmful substances' (not complete absence, mark you, but the minimum). Evidence cited elsewhere in this book will suggest that this is not always the practice of purveyors of so-called health foods. It also states that 'Artificial additives and preservatives are not to be used ... except to comply with the necessary technical and qualitative standards.' This is indeed current law – no additives may be used that are in any way harmful; those permitted are listed; and none should be used unless there is a good reason for doing so (such as complying with the necessary technical and qualitative standards!). Finally, the proposed definition of 'health foods' states that 'natural additives' are permitted – but these can be toxic, as I will explain in Chapter 2.

THE CASE FOR HEALTH FOODS

The importance of a good diet in maintaining good health has been recognized for over 2500 years, since the time when ancient Greek philosophers discussed the significant role played by diet in 'maintaining equilibrium' in the body. The doctrine of balancing waste and repair in the body is attributed to Alcmaeon of Croton, a pupil of Pythagoras, who lived in the sixth century BC. There was even a book called *Nutriment* written at the end of the fifth century BC.

So the promotion of 'health foods' over the past 150 years is by no means new. What is new is their growth.

The development of the health food movement is common to all the industrialized nations. The number of health food shops has increased markedly in all European countries, and to an even greater extent in the United States and Australia.

WHY DO WE BUY THEM?

There are many reasons for purchasing health foods – our growing interest in health, fear of unknown chemicals in our food, recommendations by semi-religious movements, hopes for a long life and sexual virility as fostered by the promotion of special preparations and our hopes for achieving super-health as well as curing diseases.

All our beliefs, fears and hopes can be played on by unscrupulous vendors of doubtful products with unproven, albeit attractive, claims. And there can be dangers in vitamin overdosage, or from plant extracts or the lack of proper quality control in small, undersupervised 'factories'.

HEALTH

In the past few years we have been made much more aware of the importance of diet in maintaining good health by the medical profession and the media. As a result, many people are wisely eating less sugar and animal fats and more poly-unsaturated fats, brown bread and dietary fibre (roughage). This has been accompanied by active exercise in the form of jogging, marathon runs, keep-fit classes and other sports.

FEAR

Some chemical substances are added to our food intentionally, and other residues are left accidentally. The former are termed food additives and are used as preservatives, colours and flavours. Unintentional residues may remain from agricultural chemicals including insecticides, fungicides and herbicides.

Intentional additives are strictly controlled by public health authorities in almost every country and it is true to say that manufactured foods have to achieve a higher standard of safety than many natural foods (as discussed in Chapter 2). Both ordinary food manufacturers and health food salesmen play on our fear of additives when declaring that their products do not contain any. Similarly we are told, incorrectly, that organically grown foods are of a superior nutritional quality.

Orthodox scientists and regulatory authorities object not to these foods, but to the claims made for them and more especially to the pills, potions, elixirs and plant extracts (of dubious value and even potential harm) that are sold alongside them.

PAIN
No one can blame an individual who is prepared to try anything in the hope of pain relief, but what is most deplorable is the way in which the purveyors of these products batten on the hopes of the sufferers and profit from their distress. When Aneurin Bevan was Minister of Health in Great Britain in 1948, the strength of public opinion compelled him to organize a clinical trial of a cancer cure that the medical profession knew did not even merit testing. In another instance, this time in the United States, vast numbers of people rushed out to buy an extract of apricot stones – wrongly called vitamin B17 – because it had been claimed to cure cancer. When its manufacture and sale were banned in some states the demand was so great that the useless extract was smuggled in from Mexico.

On a milder scale, Chapter 7 discusses slimming 'cures' and describes the continuous stream of preparations, diets and diet books that are often both useless and sufficiently dishonest as to incur legal penalties.

GOOD HEALTH, BETTER HEALTH AND SUPER HEALTH

Since food provides nourishment, promotes growth in children and keeps us alive and healthy, it is tempting to believe that we can become super healthy by eating increased amounts of the right foods. A well-trained athlete might feel he will improve his performance if he takes extra vitamins, proteins, amino acids or enzymes. If he can do this, perhaps the man in the street would also benefit from taking dietary supplements?

It is tempting to think that if one aspirin will cure a headache, then ten will stop us ever getting another one. But there is a limit to everything, and going beyond that limit does not do any good.

A severe shortage of a vitamin will cause a severe illness such as pellagra or beri-beri or failure of children to grow, and since vitamins are essential to life, the complete absence of the vitamin will lead to death. The amount needed to keep us alive is very small, only a milligram of vitamin B1 or even a microgram (a millionth of a gram) of vitamin B12, so vitamins seem to be very potent and even magical substances. Consequently it is tempting to believe that if one milligram is the margin between life and death, then 10 milligrams must lead to good health and 100 milligrams to even better, super-health.

Unfortunately this is simply not true. A motor car cannot function without a sparking plug, but its performance will not improve a jot if you carry a spare sparking plug under the bonnet!

The problem facing the nutritionist – and the individual – is to judge how much is healthy and where to draw the line, both with foods and with vitamins.

BUYING HOPE
For centuries man has sought two unattainable dreams – the Philosopher's Stone and the Elixir of Life.

The Philosopher's Stone was supposed to turn base metals into gold, and our hopes of riches beyond imagining are amply demonstrated in the betting shops, stock exchanges and race tracks of the world.

The Elixir of Life was expected to confer eternal youth, so claims for 'healthy' foods, extra and especially unknown vitamins (that is, substances called vitamins, which are not, in fact, truly vitamins), extracts of herbs and various mystical mixtures all offer most attractive prospects.

There is no evidence at present that diet can cure arthritis, poor eyesight or any other common ailment but there is always hope among those who are suffering. While there are links between our diet and some of our modern 'diseases of affluence', the remedy to these lies in modifying the whole diet, as discussed in Chapter 8, not in special foods. Sometimes people who try these special foods feel some benefit, but that may often be the power of mind over matter.

THE PLACEBO EFFECT

Around the turn of this century, aspirin tablets varied from one manufacturer to another in their purity and it was possible to say that one brand was better than another. This is no longer true – all aspirin tablets are identical now except for their price. Many people believe that paying a higher price will ensure better quality, and in the case of aspirin it is true that tablets known to be expensive will cure the headache whereas cheaper ones, if they are known to be cheap, sometimes fail to do so.

When medical drugs are under clinical trial they are always compared with something known to have no effect at all, such as coloured water. This is because some patients will show an improvement whatever they are given. This is known as the placebo effect, a term from Latin meaning 'I shall please'. The effect might be only temporary but can be real – such is the power of suggestion.

Anyone in pain who is offered relief through a 'natural' drug or health food supplement might well feel better, even if only temporarily, after taking it. It may be no more effective than tap water but he is almost certainly going to tell his friends that the new treatment helped him.

The placebo effect can work in a similar way with the vitamin supplements so heavily promoted by health food salesmen. Even people adequately supplied with vitamins from their diet may feel better after taking vitamin supplements. Although the effect wears off after a few days, the consumer may be convinced by then that the dietary supplement is essential and he will continue taking it in the belief that it is doing him good.

REVOLT AGAINST REGIMENTATION

One important reason for buying health foods is a form of revolt against regimentation. 'Health' claims include denigration of mass-produced, 'tasteless and overprocessed' foods. The term 'over-packaged' is often thrown in for good measure. Foods sweetened with honey or brown sugar instead of white sugar (although there is no difference, as is explained in Chapter 3) and organically grown foods (again no difference) become even more attractive. Health food shops also frequently stock foods not commonly available, for instance sesame seeds, buckwheat, confectionery made from dried fruit, chocolate-like products made from carob beans, sea salt and unusual fruit drinks.

Since we are all subject to numerous regulations governing our lives, purchasing the small-scale, home-made product is an acceptable form of protest against the large-scale multinational manufacturer. Health food magazines frequently denigrate conventional foods because they are mass-produced while health foods are made on so small a scale as to bear comparison with the home-made product. Even if this were once true, the business has long outgrown the concept. According to *Food Marketing Updates No. 5*, published by the Leatherhead Food Research Association in 1984, Booker Health Foods, a subsidiary of the Booker McConnell Group, exerts considerable influence over the sector through its wholesaling subsidiary, Brewhursts, and its 180 Holland and

Barrett shops. The group has six brand names including Healthcrafts which is the largest vitamin and supplement range in the UK together with Prewett's and Heath and Heather. Booker also operates a health food voluntary group called Realfare which has a membership of over 600 shops.

There is nothing wrong with such business development but it does rather contradict criticisms of reputable food firms simply because they are large.

CREDIBILITY

Would you ever believe that the 'sweat' of rocks – 'a complex mixture of organic compounds of vegetable and animal origin' – would restore health and strength to the elderly and develop male and female sexual powers? Does this claim gain credibility when you are told that the same product helps prevent digestive orders, worms, constipation, enlargement of the liver and spleen, asthma, chronic bronchitis, skin ailments, bleeding piles and anaemia?

Common sense tells us that these myriad claims cannot possibly be true, especially since we are all aware that rocks are neither animal nor vegetable but mineral. And how can any one substance achieve such diverse effects? Yet there is a product for which these claims are made – it is called Dabur Shilajit and is sold in Hong Kong.

People in the 'highly educated' Western world are unfortunately just as gullible as those who live in the Far East and subject to a much more sophisticated and advanced form of persuasive advertising. For instance, would you believe that any one product could cure arthritis, rheumatism, lumbago, high blood pressure, menopause, kidney trouble, obesity, migraine, eczema, cramp, depression, split and flaking nails, colds, bronchitis, fatigue and nervous complaints? But there is a product making such claims on sale over the counter. The reason for its efficacy over such a wide range of ailments is attributed to the fact that they all stem from 'dietary deficiency'. This can be remedied, so it is said, by an extract of two seaweeds.

Of course the seaweeds are far from ordinary: they have been 'harvested from hundreds of fathoms below the water in Norwegian fjords'. Not surprisingly the makers claim their product is remarkable. It contains twenty-eight mineral salts, twenty amino acids and fourteen vitamins. There are enough customers believing these claims to keep the product on the market.

We all know the story of the Invisible Man. H.G. Wells convinced us in half a page that such a person could exist. He explained that glass becomes invisible in water because the refractive index of water is the same as that of glass. We do not need to understand what is meant by refractive index, but we do know that glass is invisible in water. So we then believe all that follows. Therein lies the secret of a good story. All Wells' scientist had to do was change the refractive index of the human body so that it became the same as that of air and his man became invisible. It is almost believable.

So it is with health claims. The body needs zinc in small amounts and, indeed, there are a few people in the world who suffer from zinc deficiency. From this we are persuaded that everyone should buy zinc tablets – or selenium, vitamin E or copper.

We all suspect that 'Nature knows best' and therefore anything natural must by definition be better than anything artificial. Therefore a vitamin extracted by a lengthy chemical process from fruit or fish liver is thought to be superior to the identical, albeit cheaper, version synthesized in the laboratory. Milk straight from the cow, despite its possible harmful content of tubercle bacteria or streptococci, must be healthier than the homogenized, pasteurized, bottled liquid delivered to our doorstep or stocked in the supermarket.

GULLIBILITY

People frequently believe what they want to believe regardless of the facts. Dr. Rynearson of the United States quotes the result of a survey that substantiates this sad state of affairs in an article with the interesting title 'Americans Love Hogwash' (*Nutrition Reviews, July 1974*). He reports that 42 per cent of the questioned population would not regard as worthless any 'cancer cure' reported as such by scientists and doctors.

In other words they will believe what they want to despite evidence to the contrary. Furthermore only 45 per cent of the population considered that such useless treatment should be banned by law.

An even more puzzling refusal to accept the facts was put forward by Mr. Michael Wheatley in a book called *A Way of Living as a Means of Survival – An Encyclopaedia of Natural Health*. He states (p. 61), after reading a large number of books on health and disease, 'none of these books is able to qualify by scientific proof why what they say works, *and if they did I should doubt them and lose confidence in their content*' (my italics). Since he also states that he is willing to be criticized, some of his errors are pointed out in Chapter 3, but this statement is particularly relevant here.

Perhaps the layman should not be blamed for being brainwashed when qualified people are in the same position.

In a journalist's verbatim report of a farmers' protest meeting in 1965 a doctor who addressed the group is reported to have stated that farmers were being forced to produce third-rate food and that such food was probably a bigger factor in causing cancer than smoking! His speech contained such illogical statements as: 'one of a number of food dyes has been condemned as a danger by the National Union against Cancer' (from his context apparently in the United States) 'and so probably all dyes are dangerous to varying degrees.' He countered claims of insufficient evidence for his statements with the words that such an accusation 'is wearing a bit thin when there are a hundred thousand deaths in this country from cancer every year and the number is rapidly rising'. The oratory may be powerful but the logic is non-existent.

Twenty years later there is still no clear evidence that any item in the diet can cause cancer. If a qualified doctor can make such statements to the public, how can we be blamed for listening to the views of 'health food' purveyors?

ASSESSING THE WRITTEN AND SPOKEN WORD

One major problem then is how to find the facts. Many health magazines may sound plausible, but when their claims are laid side by side they begin to lack credibility.

When reading a book or article on health foods, try first to ascertain the qualifications, if any, of the author. A certain standard of scientific qualification usually suggests that the author knows what he is talking about, but this is not always true. A book on nutrition written by a doctor in 1936 stated, for example, that 'a vitamin is something that never has been and never will be synthesized'. Several vitamins had already been synthesized by then in the laboratory and one or two had even been manufactured. The same book advocates separating out fats, carbohydrates and proteins in food to reduce weight, a task that is not only unnecessary but also impossible as explained later.

Some of the books that advocate special lifestyles are undoubtedly written in good faith, but others are so far-fetched and nonsensical that it is difficult to believe their authors had any goal other than to mislead, and make a profit from, a gullible public.

THE PHYSIOLOGICAL ASPECT

Curiously, some of these authors appear to invent their own physiology as well. Physiology is the study of the way in which the body works – the digestion of food, circulation of the blood, functioning of the liver and kidneys and so on. It has been studied for centuries and while there are always new things being discovered about how the body works, the basic facts are well known. We all study physiology at school and there are hundreds of simple textbooks explaining it. Yet some authors do not use existing knowledge, but invent their own 'science'.

For example, in *The Beverly Hills Diet* the author reports 'a great discovery' – that the body contains three enzymes (one of which is hydrochloric acid). In fact, the body contains several thousand enzymes, each carrying out a particular function. Every elementary book of physiology and biochemistry describes these in great detail.

Another interesting item of physiology is that each type of food – fat, protein and carbohydrate – is digested by a different group of digestive enzymes (true) so you must therefore avoid mixing them together (untrue). Such advice is not only incorrect, it is also impossible to follow because nearly all foods are mixtures. Bread, for instance, contains carbohydrates, protein and fat as well as several vitamins and minerals. Meat contains fat and protein. Milk contains all three in roughly equal amounts. Even without knowing about human physiology we can tell that such advice is absurd – we eat all these foods all the time with no adverse effects.

In the same book there are three separate statements which are obviously nonsensical, even more so when they are placed side by side:

1 carbohydrates fester, ferment and rot in the stomach;
2 melba toast turns to alcohol in the stomach;
3 potatoes are fermented into vodka in the stomach.

In another 'invention' the thymus gland, which is in the chest, is credited with producing the enzymes that digest milk. How the enzyme, which the gland does not in fact contain, could get from the chest to the stomach is left to the imagination. The thymus actually produces some of the body's defence systems (lymphocytes) and is not concerned with digestion in any way.

Since there are so many books, both scientific works and popular paperbacks, available on physiology, it is difficult to understand why the authors of crank books persist in inventing their own forms of science. One would have thought that the true facts were sufficiently sensational to attract readers.

Chemistry can be equally novel in such books. We are told, for example, that hydrochloric acid in the stomach breaks down fat. Chemistry shows us that the two do not even mix together. Heating foods such as milk and eggs is said to destroy lecithin, a substance quite stable to heat.

Many diet books advocate eating raw food as a source of enzymes. In fact, although raw fruit and vegetables do contain many enzymes, these are inherent to the plants and are of no use to us. As enzymes are proteins, they are simply digested like any other protein in our diet. The potential dangers of eating raw foods are discussed in Chapter 2.

Some contradictions are obvious as, for example, 'dietary fibre must never be eaten with starch' followed by the advice that 'fibre-enriched bread rolls' are 'healthy food'.

While some foods have been incorrectly promoted as cures for certain diseases, such as arthritis and cancer, other authors relate specific foods to different parts of the body. We are told that the kidneys are stimulated by beans, green vegetables and chestnuts; the lungs by peaches, onions and rice; the pancreas by millet and dates, and so on. In fact, all foods follow the same process of digestion and absorption and have no particular effect on any special part of the body. Carbohydrates (i.e. starches and sugars) are digested to their simplest unit, glucose. This enters the bloodstream and feeds every tissue in the body. In a similar way, all fats are broken down and enter the bloodstream as their component parts, the fatty acids and glycerol, or are absorbed as droplets of unchanged fat. The mixture also travels around the body to all tissues.

Similarly all proteins, whether from vegetables or animal foods, are digested to their constituent parts, the amino acids. These enter the bloodstream and go to every organ in the body to be used there. The liver does get first choice since the blood from the intestines carrying our food supplies goes first to the liver before joining the whole blood circulation system. So it is absurd to claim that any foodstuff stimulates one organ or tissue more than another.

Nor is it true to say that meat makes you aggressive, that milk clogs up the digestive tract or that fruit gives you peace. So the search for the true facts can be found by comparing the facts that are given in all standard textbooks with the 'facts' that have been invented.

SCIENCE OR SALESMANSHIP?

Scientists have discovered factors at various times which they thought were essential to life and have called them vitamins. Later these were proved not to be dietary essentials, therefore not vitamins, and of little or no importance to the diet. Examples are vitamins B13, B14, B15 and B17. These are not vitamins but are chemical substances of no particular value to us. Since they were once incorrectly or accidentally labelled vitamins, however, health food salesmen persist in using this status as a selling claim.

There are many substances in the diet which are useful but which can be made by the body from other parts of the diet – these include choline, inositol, substances in orange peel called flavonoids and made to sound more important by being called bioflavonoids, and lecithin. Even enzymes, which the body always makes for itself, are sold as food supplements with claims for their special virtues. All of these substances are present in food but they sound sufficiently scientific to carry conviction.

Often a tentative suggestion in a research paper is seized upon as proven fact in order to sell a product. Among the many theories of what causes aging is one which suggests, without much evidence, that it results from the oxidation (rancidity) of the fatty materials from which cell walls are made. Since both vitamin E and vitamin C are antioxidants (fat preservatives) and are indeed used as such in the food manufacturing industry, they are sold as 'geriatric vitamins' with claims that they will lengthen life and stave off old age. A good story, but not a strictly honest one.

WHAT IS WRONG WITH THESE PRODUCTS?

Once against it must be pointed out that there is nothing wrong with most of the food sold in health food shops. The cause for concern lies in the claims made for them and, in particular, for the pills, potions and herbal remedies offered at such shops. There are, however, some risks of harm:

1 vitamin overdosage;
2 toxic supplements such as laetrile (so-called vitamin B17);
3 toxic herbal preparations and plant extracts;
4 malnutrition from fad diets;
5 cash loss, especially to the elderly and less affluent;
6 misinformation and brainwashing.

These problems are discussed in detail later but two require emphasis at the outset. The first is the dangerous practice of recommending cures for diseases that require medical attention. If treatment is delayed or abandoned in favour of self-medication, whether with exotic food preparations or mystical and inaccurately labelled vitamins, the results can be fatal. Indeed there have been reports in the medical journals of lives lost for this very reason.

The second is the large and growing power of advertising claims which sound attractive but which bear no relation to the facts and often result in brainwashing. Between their hopes and the scientific sounding claims made, some addicts no longer want to listen to facts. They have unshakeable faith in products such as cider vinegar, seaweed, herbal extracts or unusual foods.

PARADISE LOST

As part of our revolt against regimentation and anger against pollution and damage to the environment, many of us want to go back to 'things as they were' and 'return to nature'. Unfortunately man began to interfere with nature at least 10,000 years ago when he began to cultivate crops instead of continuing as a hunter-gatherer, so it is far too late to 'go back'. Nevertheless, claims for the Garden of Eden, Paradise and Natural Man all bolster the belief in health foods.

Sylvester Graham, an American dietitian in the nineteenth century, pioneered the use of flour made from whole grain as long ago as 1840. Whole grain flour is, as explained elsewhere, nutritionally superior to white flour. In other respects, however, Graham epitomized the nonsense so often given out by 'health' food salesmen.

FOOD PREJUDICES AND TABOOS
(Graham 1794–1851)

Food should not be consumed when hot
Water should not be consumed with meals
Tea causes delirium tremens
Condiments and sexual excess cause insanity
Chicken pie and lewdness cause cholera
Meat consumption causes sin

When Graham stated that 'in all probability the diet of our forebears in the Garden of Eden was fruit, nuts, farinaceous seeds and roots with perhaps some milk and maybe honey', he thought that he knew what was good for us. But how can anyone know what was eaten in that hypothetical place? The statement is so completely absurd that no one could be expected to give it credence. Yet Graham was not trying to sell anything – he was simply stating his views of what he believed, probably quite sincerely, to be a healthy diet.

THE POWER OF THE MEDIA

It seems that scientific fact not only fails to shake public belief in miracle cures, but also fails to shake public distrust once it has been awakened. The example of the food additive E330 is a case in point. The campaign against E330 began in France six years ago, spread to Belgium and more recently Italy despite some very simple facts.

The story begins in 1974 with a letter, ostensibly from a Paris hospital, Villejuif, which listed 139 chemical additives permitted in foods by the 'uncaring bureaucrats' of the Common Market. Some were described as inoffensive, twenty-seven were called suspect and eighteen were called toxic. Thirteen were described as carcinogenic, with one, E330, being the most dangerous of all.

The letter was immediately written up in the Press and public concern in France spread rapidly. The problem got so out of hand that the French Minister of Agriculture had to make a statement to the Senate in July 1976 to explain that E330 was simply citric acid, a perfectly harmless substance found in many foods. The government was, he said, trying to find the perpetrator of the hoax. This did not end the matter, however, and the French Ministry of Health issued another statement in 1978.

E330, mysterious as it sounds, is simply an EEC classification number. Of all the substances that can be described as 'natural' and harmless, the one that most merits these titles is citric acid. It is not only present in most fruits, especially the citrus fruits from which it gets its name, but is also produced in every cell in the human body. Cells use glucose as their source of energy and this goes through twenty-one stages as it is being burned up until it finishes as carbon dioxide and water, releasing energy along the way. Stage number nineteen is the formation of citric acid – a discovery that won the Nobel Prize.

The classification number is no more mysterious than the colour that is used in Great Britain under the cloak of Brown FK. The letters in this instance mean For Kippers.

Despite all the evidence the story not only persisted, but spread subsequently to Belgium where an official denial had to be issued by the Ministry of Public Health and Environment in 1979. The story was still going the rounds in 1982 and had spread to Italy.

THE OFFICIAL VIEW

The (British) Food Standards Committee in its 1980 *Report on Claims and Misleading Descriptions* stated:

> *'In a general sense all food can be considered as health-giving in that lack of the right amounts of a sufficient variety eventually results in bad health. To this extent the term "health" applied to any foods is a superfluous and misleading description but it is generally used to imply an extra health-giving quality which "ordinary" food does not possess; some of the claims made for this "extra" quality stray into areas of nutrition about which there may still be insufficient knowledge and yet others may be pure fantasy.*

> *'Some of these customers could be deceived more readily' (than customers who consider they have some, but often unorthodox, knowledge of nutrition) 'because their interest in diet made them more susceptible to claims that a particular food was "good" or "bad" for their wellbeing ... The increasing sales of these foods through other types of retail outlet, including pharmacies, and the growing number of "health" claims made for normal foods must be a matter for concern.'*

The Association of Public Analysts in its 1983 report stated:

> *'During the year a survey has been carried out to establish the extent of surveillance of the so-called "health foods" although it should be recognized that this meaningless term does not indicate that such foods are special or subject to constraints other than those of normal food legislation. Undeclared preservatives in dried fruit and infestation of dried fruits have been found. The existence of aflatoxins in some samples of nuts has already been mentioned ... Action has been taken ... examples include some high fibre tablets, so-called "starch blockers", super body builders and compound vitamin preparations.'*

Further evidence has been published that organically grown foods do not taste any better than other food, are not healthier and do not prevent cancer. 'There is no difference from ordinary foods in the generally low pesticide residue level; the only difference is price.'

In a debate on health foods organized by the (British) Institute of Food Science and Technology in 1984 a public analyst complained of the 'holier than thou' attitude of health food promoters who claim that their foods are made from high quality raw materials, implying that other foods are not. He had, however, as a public analyst, examined many cases of fruits and vegetables from health food shops and found them to be infested with insects, had found belladonna as a contaminant in herbal teas, and had found toxins in nuts.

Errors have been made, such as claims that foods were free of preservatives when sulphur dioxide was found in them and was not listed on the label. Other errors include tablets of 'natural' vitamins, presumably extracted from foods as distinct from those manufactured in the laboratory, which included vitamin D2 on the label. This is the synthetic form which rarely occurs in nature – the natural form is vitamin D3. Both are equally useful to human begins, so this was probably a simple error, but it was obviously not noticed as it has continued for many years.

Finally, an article on health foods in the magazine *Which?* (*June 1978*) states that health food devotees believe such foods to be superior to ordinary supermarket foods because they are supposedly whole, unprocessed, free from added colours, flavours and preservatives, and organically grown. All these aspects are discussed fully later in the book. The article concludes by saying that: 'We could find no clear differences between most "health food" brands and other comparable brands of beans, peas, lentils, seeds, sugars, drinks, nuts, yeast extracts, yoghurts, herbs, honey and spices.' The article also denies the curative properties of what the magazine calls 'wonder foods' – such as royal jelly, pollen, cider vinegar, yoghurt, wheatgerm, pollen, molasses, honey, brewers' yeast and kelp – all of which have been said to be capable of making

21

you glow with health, stating: 'We know of no scientifically acceptable evidence of miracle cures brought about by these wonder foods.'

INVENT A NEW HEALTH PRODUCT

It is not difficult to see why people are persuaded to buy things – after all, this is the stock-in-trade of the advertiser. It is relatively easy to invent products and indeed, as discussed later in the chapter on slimming 'cures', almost any novel idea can be made to seem credible.

As an example of such an invention, consider a purely mythical product called Father Cohen's Miracle Cure. The religious connotation, biblical reference and term 'miracle' provide a good start to convincing the audience. In its descriptive leaflet, the opening paragraph reveals what few scientists know, namely that the almond has particularly valuable properties. As evidence, it is said that Aaron's rod was an almond branch and that the ancient Romans considered the almond nut to be both an aphrodisiac (always a winner) and a cure for madness. Anything ancient is considered better than its modern equivalent but if you combine its antiquity with the modern scientific method of extracting the vital principle – unspecified – you can produce a real moneyspinner.

People are actually buying 'the active principle of eighteen oysters' from sex shops despite the fact that it does not exist, so why wouldn't they buy Father Cohen's Miracle Cure?

2

NATURE KNOWS
BEST?

NATURAL – USAGE AND ABUSAGE

The word 'natural' is used in so many connotations by the advertisers of traditional as well as health foods that it has lost all meaning and ought to be banned. Indeed, there have been suggestions from time to time to control its use.

In a *Report of the British Food Standards Committee (Claims and Misleading Descriptions 1966)* it was recommended that the word natural should only be used without qualification in two senses. First, to indicate that ingredients (such as colours and flavours) were extracted from biological material as distinct from being synthetic. Second, to mean unprocessed and without any additions.

'Pure' was also discussed and it was recommended that its use should be restricted to products which contain no additive of any kind. (It is difficult to see where chemically impure sea salt fits here compared with chemically purified salt from salt mines, see page 94.)

In 1983 the Canadian Department for Consumer and Corporate Affairs suggested guidelines pertaining to the use of the term 'natural' to describe a food or its ingredients (*Communiqué No. 38*). This was considered necessary to safeguard the significance of the term 'since it is deemed important to consumers'.

It was suggested that the term should be restricted to foods 'which have been submitted to a minimum of processing and which have undergone a minimum of physical, chemical or biological change'. Such a definition differs with the opinions of different manufacturers, retailers and consumers, and the guidelines have not met with general approval. Baking, for example, was listed as non-significant despite the major changes in physical properties and nutritional damage to protein quality and vitamin B1 that inevitably accompany baking of any degree or type. Degerming was also listed among the insignificant changes but many consumers would certainly not accept that.

The guidelines did not permit use of the word for a food that had been simply enriched with vitamins and minerals. Presumably milk straight from the cow is a natural food, but what if the diet of the cow has been manipulated? It is possible to increase the vitamin A in milk by feeding extra to the cow, and it is possible to increase the vitamin D by exposing the milk to sunshine.

With such difficulties it might be more advisable to ban any use of the word.

The appeal of the term natural to the consumer is obvious but it can be misused unintentionally or innocently. For example a book of 'natural cooking' (if cooking itself can be considered natural), extolled 'natural brandy' – made by fermenting grape juice and then distilling it – but said that fortified wines – made by fermenting the grape juice and then adding previously distilled brandy – are 'unnatural and bad'.

ADVERTISING

The term natural is used in advertising in four different ways. The first means a food taken from the ground, sea or farm and not processed in any way. So all raw fruits, vegetables, farm crops, meat, fish and milk would fall into this category. Such definitions would seem to be in the minds of health food purveyors when they describe ordinary foods as refined, tinned, frozen, freeze-dried, excessively packaged (which is in some way a derogatory term) and 'otherwise tampered with'.

This is to distinguish unprocessed foods from those to which colours, flavours and preservatives have been added, or which have been subjected to any treatment listed above. It is not made clear at what temperature a food ceases to be regarded as natural – in the above description of processed foods, processing is clearly denigrated but it is not clear whether cooling in a refrigerator or exposure to cold weather is equally deprecated.

A speaker on BBC Woman's Hour once discussed how she would never have a refrigerator, but was living in Scotland and had a north-facing larder. In her mind it was clear that artificial cold differed from natural cold.

A second use of the word is simply for the commercial purpose of making a product appear superior to that of a rival. Butter, for instance, is advertised as being natural while margarine adverts say it is made from natural ingredients. Both, of course, are equally true. Butter is made from a product, milk, that must, under all headings, be considered as natural, but it has to be manipulated by separating the cream, churning, often adding salt and colouring matter (which can come from a plant extract or even be synthetic). Whether or not it can still be called natural is arguable. Similarly margarine is made from oils extracted from natural sources such as nuts, fish and animal carcasses, hardened with hydrogen in the presence of a nickel catalyst, salted, coloured and enriched with vitamins.

In the public mind butter is regarded as the more natural product although nutritionally margarine may be the same as, or, as I will explain later, even superior to butter. Both are claimed as natural for advertising purposes.

A third use of the word is again for commercial reasons when the food has been processed to a lesser degree than its rival. So brown sugar, which has been highly purified from the starting material, whether beet or cane, is labelled natural compared to white sugar which is fractionally more refined. Sea salt, 98 per cent pure sodium chloride, is labelled 'natural sea salt' and sometimes 'pure, natural sea salt' as distinct from the very pure recrystallized product which is 99 per cent sodium chloride. The difference between the 98 per cent and 99 per cent is largely debris from the sea such as particles of shrimp, fish and seaweed. These will provide a trace of mineral salts but too little to be of any nutritional interest. The 'dirt' is not harmful but is invariably costly.

The fourth use of the word is in distinction from artificial or substitute. The latter sounds inferior to the real thing, but this is not necessarily so in terms of convenience or usefulness for its purpose. For example, to anyone interested in drip dry clothes that do not need ironing, man-made substitutes are superior to natural cotton, wool or linen. To those who object to killing animals for decoration, artificial fur is superior to the real thing. For hygienic reasons, laboratory synthesized, factory-made plastic surfaces are superior for food preparation to wood which is porous.

Health food shops sell natural vitamins with claims that they are superior to those synthesized in a factory, but this is untrue. The lengthy and complicated chemical processes involved in extracting a vitamin from a food result in a product which is identical in every way with that produced in the factory. If this were not so then the chemist would have failed in the task set him by the nutritionist. This is a clear case of natural versus synthetic, but it is of no nutritional significance – the synthetic product is usually cheaper.

Margarine was originally invented as a poor man's substitute for butter. It is nutritionally superior since it has more (added) vitamin D than butter and can be made with polyunsaturated fatty acids compared with the saturated type present in butter and considered to be harmful in relation to coronary heart disease.

Coffee whitener is grossly inferior nutritionally to milk but far more convenient for use, say, in an office. Artificial sweeteners are superior to sugar if the latter plays any part in supplying unwanted calories or damaging the teeth.

So natural, meaning the real thing compared with the artificial or substitute, may not always be superior.

Just to complete the picture, there were eggs on sale for

many years in Great Britain labelled 'natural' – presumably from their real parents!

MAN'S NATURAL FOOD

There is yet another use of the term natural in the context of a food that is natural for man to eat. Such a food is even more difficult to define. Many articles have been written to explain why man is naturally a vegetarian because of the construction of his intestines, just as many others have argued that he is a carnivore because primitive man was a hunter. It is not possible to prove either argument and in practice human beings are omnivores – we eat almost everything.

In the context of what is natural food, the term is often applied to whole foods as distinct from processed or refined foods. Compare wholemeal bread with white bread for instance. Certainly wholemeal bread contains more nutrients, but what is natural about separating the wheat grain from the rest of the plant, grinding it, adding a strange living substance called yeast, usually together with salt, mixing it with water and leaving it to ferment, then subjecting it to so high a temperature that a great deal of the vitamin B1 and the amino acid lysine are destroyed?

There is no food other than mother's milk that can be considered as natural for human beings, and even that suits only babies. While there is no doubt that breast milk is best for babies it is not always realized that its nutrient composition can vary with the mother's diet, especially in its vitamin content. There is even a report in the *New England Journal of Medicine (Vol. 299, 1978)* of anaemia developing in a breast-fed infant because the mother was a strict vegetarian who consumed no vitamin B12. So what can be called man's natural food?

SAFETY AND TOXICITY OF FOODS

Since most of our foods are pasteurized, sterilized, canned, bottled, homogenized and otherwise processed, as well as being chemically preserved, coloured and flavoured, it is quite understandable that people are often concerned. We are entitled to ask whether such foods are safe to eat and whether 'natural' unprocessed foods are not better.

In fact, food laws take care of the safety of manufactured foods and no chemical aids are permitted unless they are considered to be safe. So far from unprocessed foods being safer than factory products, the opposite is true because processed foods have to satisfy certain standards while raw fruit, vegetables, fish and meat do not.

An interesting example which would test the lawyers is the case of the fruit from Scandinavia known as cloudberry. This fruit, rather like a yellow raspberry in appearance but sharply acid in taste, is so rich in the natural preservative benzoic acid that it cannot ferment and does not go bad. It will keep fresh – if that is the right word – for years.

Benzoic acid is a permitted preservative for fruit juices in Great Britain but in strictly limited amounts. Fruit squashes and cordials which are to be diluted with water before being served may contain not more than 800 parts per million of benzoic acid. If the fruit juice preparation is ready-to-drink without adding water, then it must not contain more than one-fifth of this amount, i.e. 160 parts per million, which is 0.016 per cent.

In their natural state, cloudberries contain as much as 0.8 per cent benzoic acid which is eight thousand parts per million or fifty times the legal limit!

There is no law to stop anyone selling cloudberries because they are a 'natural' food. They grow wild in abundance in Finland and any manufacturer could prepare and sell a mixture of orange juice and cloudberry juice which would contain more than the legal limit of preservative without breaking the law because the benzoic acid came from a natural food!

In Japan and the surrounding countries, about 200 people die each year from eating Puffer fish (tetraodontin poisoning). The fish have a poison sac which must be carefully removed –

restaurants serving it have certified chefs to prepare the fish – because if even a small amount of the poison spills onto the fish it becomes toxic. If people died after eating any manufactured product that product would quickly be banned, but because the fish are 'natural' they continue to be sold and consumed.

PROCESSING AIDS

Chemicals are added to foods during processing for a variety of reasons – to colour, flavour and preserve. When foods are made with fats and watery ingredients which do not normally mix, then a variety of emulsifiers are used to enable them to mix, and other substances, called stabilizers, are used to maintain the emulsion. Emulsifiers and stabilizers allow oil and water to mix in mayonnaise and ice cream, as well as providing the smooth texture of chocolate and other similar foods.

In addition, there are substances that are generally helpful such as anti-caking agents added to salt and other powders. This can be of assistance to manufacturers since many of the ingredients in modern large-scale factories are blown along pipes in powder form into mixing vessels.

Another convenient additive is an anti-spattering agent which is put into frying oils. When wet fish or chipped potatoes are put into very hot oil the water boils off so quickly that it has the force of an explosion and many housewives used to finish frying their chips with burns on their arms from the hot oil. A fat-derivative called lecithin, among others, is added to frying oil to emulsify the water into such small droplets that they boil off without the sudden explosive effect.

The necessity and relative importance of these additives differ. Preservatives play an important role not only in helping to keep foods which would otherwise go bad but in preventing the growth of harmful bacteria. Colours are open to argument. While they are often merely cosmetic and unnecessary, they are often used to please the consumer. Some years ago a leading firm of retailers in Great Britain decided to discontinue the addition of the traditional green colour to their canned peas and the red colour to strawberry jam and canned strawberries – all of which change during processing. The result was greenish-grey peas, brownish jam turning dull brown after a few months, and straw-coloured strawberries. Customers immediately reacted by asking what was 'wrong' with the foods. Sales of these products fell by half. By the time the colours were restored, the public had lost so much faith in the company that it took two years for sales to regain their previous level.

Colours are added to cakes and biscuits, sugar confectionery, soft drinks, jellies, canned fruits and vegetables, ice cream, butter and cheese. Much of our enjoyment of food depends on eye appeal, although the addition of colours is not essential and is less important than preservatives. So apart from preservatives, the addition of chemicals is largely for convenience and attraction.

Altogether several thousand chemical aids are added to food. This may sound alarming, but no one in Great Britain has ever suffered harm from an intentional additive. In fact, the only report of harm from an additive was in 1967 when a cobalt salt was added to beer in Canada, the United States and Belgium to increase the head of froth. There were several cases of fatal heart disease which ceased when cobalt was banned. This is the only known case of harm from an intentional additive so far as we know. Some people are intolerant or allergic to certain additives, but no more than are intolerant of foods such as strawberries, melons, meat fat, cheese and many other foods.

The fact that many additives have been banned indicates the care taken by toxicologists in this area. Bans result from animal experiments when large doses indicate harm but none of these banned substances has ever been shown to harm human beings. Clearly, we do not want to consume chemicals that harm animals and prefer to ban them before any effects come to light in human beings.

The very word chemical is emotive despite the fact that all

our foodstuffs, fat, proteins, carbohydrates, vitamins and mineral salts as well as we ourselves, are chemicals.

Unprocessed natural foods contain very large numbers of chemicals that go to make up their particular taste and texture. If we had to label our fruit saying what it contained, it would look horrifying. An apple, for example, contains 230 chemical substances in the flavour alone and an orange contains 330. These include acids (such as formic and acetic acids and 20 others), alcohols (up to 30 or 40 in number), esters such as ethyl acetate (numbering about 100), carbonyls (such as formaldehyde and acetaldehyde) and many others.

Some of the additives in processed foods have been used for centuries – e.g. spices, sugar and salt used as preservatives. Some are the same chemical substances that are formed in the body from our diet. One, for example, with the fearsome name of glyceryl monostearate, is formed during the digestion of ordinary dietary fats. It is a non-greasy flexible substance used to keep bread soft (an anti-staling agent). It is also used as an anti-spattering agent. Other substances formed normally in the body and also used as food additives include lactic acid, pyruvic acid and citric acid.

Some additives are extracted from foods, others are synthesized in the laboratory. An interesting one that has been used as a red colouring over the centuries is cochineal. This is extracted from the female conchilla insect; it takes 70,000 insects to produce 1 lb of red colour. Imagine inventing that today. Turmeric, used in pickles, curry powder and prepared mustard both as a flavour and yellow colour, is the dried root (rhizome) of a plant of the ginger family. Butter is coloured with annatto (also called bixin or butter yellow) extracted from the seed pods of a plant, Bixa orellana.

If a colour, flavour or preservative has been extracted from a food it must be tested for safety before it can be used as an additive. Yet the original food containing such substances can be freely sold because unprocessed foods are not subject to legal control. So it is true to say that processed foods can be safer than raw, natural, unprocessed foods.

HOW SAFE ARE UNPROCESSED FOODS?

Unprocessed foods which produce ill-effects fall into four groups. First there are poisonous berries, mushrooms, foods never seen in Western countries such as the lathyrus pea, ackee fruit and cycad seeds, as well as various seafoods which become highly toxic at certain times of the year as a result of their own diet. This group is outside the present discussion.

The second group consists of foods that adversely affect only a few individuals – generally covered by the term allergy and also outside a discussion of health food claims.

The third group is made up of foods that contain substances known to be toxic but usually in small and harmless amounts.

The fourth group comprises ordinary foods or nutrients which are not only good for us but also some, such as vitamins, which are essential to life, yet which are toxic when eaten in excess.

Anyone who reads detective novels knows that cyanide is a poison but few people know that vitamin A is even more poisonous as will be discussed on page 154. More than 100 cases of vitamin A poisoning in children have been discussed in the medical literature – they were given excessive doses of cod or halibut liver oil over a period of several weeks – and a total of nearly 600 cases have been reported.

Vitamin D is even more toxic than vitamin A, as will be discussed on page 154. It is interesting, if not worrying, to know that cyanide is found in sorghum (a favourite health food), butter beans, cassava (a staple food in many African countries) and millet. It is also found in the Czech liqueur called Slivovitz from the cherry stones used to make it.

The minimum lethal dose of cyanide is estimated at 35–250 mg; you would have to eat 1–7 lb of white butter beans to feel the effects, so they are fairly harmless. But there are some coloured varieties of butter beans – like the Puerto Rican Black – which contain thirty times as much cyanide, and as little as ½–3½ oz would be fatal. Needless to say we do not eat these.

The reason we can consume these foods without any ill-effects is that the amounts of poison are small enough for the body to deal with between meals and they do not accumulate in the body. Cassava does contain large amounts of cyanide but it is removed during the traditional grinding preparation when an enzyme naturally present is allowed to liberate the cyanide which then evaporates.

Caffeine is a well-known stimulant which we all drink in tea and coffee. There is enough caffeine in 20 cups of coffee to kill a man. So in four or five days, many of us drink a fatal dose of caffeine, but the body disposes of it. Salt is essential to life: 1–2 g of sodium is as essential as any vitamin, yet 100 g of salt (about 40 g of sodium) is a lethal dose. Even water, surely as natural and essential for life as anything one can imagine, is lethal if large amounts are taken. Three litres drunk in 20 minutes have been shown to be lethal. Clearly, too much of anything, natural or otherwise, can be harmful.

NATURAL TOXINS

Almost every natural unprocessed vegetable contains harmful substances, although in small amounts. There is oxalic acid in spinach, potatoes, watercress, parsley, coriander and even lettuce although no one has yet died of a surfeit of lettuce – so far as we know.

The list of harmful substances found in nature is almost limitless. Sweet potatoes contain ipomearone (which damages the liver and lungs), mace and nutmeg contain myristin (which causes hallucinations and if eaten in quantity by pregnant women can affect the baby in the womb). This chemical is even found in bananas, parsnips, celery, black pepper and fennel.

The enormous number of toxic compounds in food is exemplified by a group of chemicals called pyrrolizidine alkaloids. About 150 of these are found in a wide variety of plants eaten by animals. These compounds then enter the human food chain through meat, milk and cheese as well as being present in cereal grains and honey. The substances are lethal when fed to experimental animals in large amounts.

They damage the liver and the cardio-pulmonary system as well as causing cancer and they are all natural. But in the amounts in our food they cause no harm – as far as we know.

Man, in a joint effort between scientists and farmers, sometimes administers oestrogens, female sex hormones, to cattle to increase the yield of meat simply for profit. This may sound reprehensible but a vast number of plants naturally contain oestrogens – soy beans, Mexican yams, carrots, potatoes, cherries, plums, garlic, parsley, green beans, peanuts, wheat, rice, oats, barley and even ordinary apples.

THE HUMBLE POTATO

Of all the foods that might be considered natural, at the forefront is the ordinary potato. Apart from canned, dried, frozen and otherwise processed potatoes, we eat vast quantities boiled, roasted, as French fries, as crisps (called chips in most other countries) and in a wide variety of other dishes. The average Briton eats 125 lb (57 kg) a year and some people as much as 600 lb.

Yet potatoes contain a highly toxic substance called solanine. Solanine acts by damaging the nerve stimulators (choline esterase) in a similar way to war gases. The symptoms include drowsiness, mental confusion, trembling and sometimes vomiting and fever. One might well ask how it is possible to eat so common a food in such large amounts if it really does contain poisonous substances. The answer is that the amount present is small enough to be dealt with by the body before the next meal comes along, so we are really quite safe.

Normally 100 g of potato contains only 3–6 mg of solanine, a perfectly safe amount. When they sprout or are exposed to light and turn green, the solanine increases to harmful levels and cases have been reported of people eating potatoes with about ten times this amount. In the *Lancet (29 September 1979)*, with reference to 78 schoolboys in South London who were taken ill after eating green potatoes, the author wondered why solanine poisoning from potatoes was not more common, and suggested that it might, indeed, be more common than we realize but is just not recognized.

WATERCRESS AND BRUSSELS SPROUTS

There are a number of vegetables which have a pungent taste, slightly burning and bitter on the tongue. Some, like mustard and horseradish, are very hot; others, like watercress and Brussels sprouts, are only slightly bitter. These foods contain a group of chemicals called vinyl-OZT (short for vinyl oxazolidine thione). When the tissue is broken down during chewing, these compounds are changed into chemicals that have the hot, pungent taste. They are called allyl-CNS (short for allyl isothiocyanates).

The legal requirements in Great Britain for what are called mustard condiments state that they must yield a certain amount of allyl-CNS after macerating with water for 2 hours at 37 degrees C. At least 80 different vinyl-OZT compounds are found in foods, which give them their different flavours.

In fact, all the cabbage family, which includes cauliflower, swedes, turnips and Brussels sprouts, as well as cabbage itself and the radish family (Cruciferae) which includes kohl-rabi, broccoli, watercress, mustard and horseradish, as well as the ordinary radish, all contain these chemicals.

Apart from the pungent taste, allyl-CNS and vinyl-OZT are toxic. As far as the plants are concerned, they offer protection from insects, bacteria and fungi. As far as we are concerned, their taste is pleasant. But the fact remains that here are natural unprocessed foods, coming straight from the ground and not passing through any factory, yet containing substances known to be toxic. Of course no one has died from a surfeit of watercress or cabbage – so far as we know – but then no one in this country has died from an intentional food additive – so far as we know.

When food additives are tested for safety they are fed to experimental animals in very high doses for several months, then the animals are killed and their tissues and organs examined for any changes. Normal practice is to take the highest dose that has *no effect* on the animals and then permit one-hundredth of this amount to be added to food.

When vinyl-OZT and allyl-CNS are consumed in high doses they interfere with the growth of animals and damage the thyroid, liver and kidneys. With such effects, no public health authority would permit their use but because they are present in natural foods and we have eaten them for such a long time, the cabbage and radish families of vegetables could hardly be banned. The practical question is whether eating these (natural) foods could really cause any harm.

It is difficult to find out exactly how much would cause harm because people differ. But there are some figures from people who volunteered to consume these 'natural' chemicals. Two Viennese workers reported that a dose of 100–400 mg of OZT daily for periods of 5 days to 6 months damaged the thyroid gland (*Further Advances in Thyroid Research by Peltola and Krusius, edited by Fellinger and Hofer for the Vienna Medical Academy, 1971, pp. 149–153*). Another laboratory found that a single dose of 25 mg was effective in damaging the thyroid (*Langer, Endocrinology, 1971, vol. 57, pp. 225–229*).

But how much do we eat in our vegetables? The answer came from the UK Food Research Institute (*Journal of the Science of Food and Agriculture 1984*). It was found that in winter, when Britons eat considerable amounts of Brussels sprouts, the average intake is 60 mg daily – certainly in the harmful range. In summer, when we eat fewer sprouts and more cabbage, the daily intake falls to 30 mg. These are, of course, averages and the authors suggest that some people will be consuming as much as 300 mg daily.

There is no evidence that even Brussels sprout or cabbage addicts suffer harm but these findings demonstrate that so-called natural, fresh vegetables, untouched by human hand, are 'worse' than processed, manufactured foods which are more strictly controlled by law. After all, it would be more than difficult to exercise legal control over the radish or cauliflower.

Those chemicals present in natural foods are nothing to do with fertilizers, artificial or otherwise. They are simply formed in the plant for its protection, and we happen to like eating them.

ORGANIC FARMING

Along with the belief that natural unprocessed foods must be harmless and, indeed, beneficial, comes the belief that organic fertilizers, i.e. animal manure or vegetable compost, are more suitable for growing plants than inorganic salts such as sulphate of ammonia, superphosphate or potash which come from the chemical factory.

The latter are often called artificial fertilizers but the titles are back to front. It is the organic material that is artificial because plants can only use inorganic salts. Manure and compost are excellent conditioners and help retain moisture in the soil, but the nutrients they contain cannot be used by the plant until they have been broken down to inorganic salts by the microorganisms in the soil. Sulphate of ammonia and other inorganic fertilizers are ready for the plant to use, so they are really the natural ones.

Claims are made that crops grown with organic fertilizers are more nutritious and tasty. Taste will be discussed later, in Chapter 4, but there have been a few investigations into nutritional value which are relevant here.

In a trial conducted by the Royal Veterinary College of London, mice were fed on wheat which was grown for ten successive generations on soil that had been treated only with chemical fertilizers. They were compared with a second group, fed on wheat grown on soil treated with compost and a third, fed on wheat grown under what are more usual farming conditions, that is, a mixture of dung and chemical fertilizers (*Journal of Reproduction and Fertility, May 1960*). The results did not show any difference. To be precise, out of 17 pairs of breeding mice on each diet, the 'artificial' fertilizer group gave birth to 37 babies, of which 28 survived weaning; those fed organically manured wheat gave birth to 39 babies, with only 22 surviving weaning. So the inorganic wheat was slightly better, but the difference was too small to be conclusive. What the experiment really showed was that wheat alone is not a very good diet because mice fed on standard laboratory mixed rations gave birth to 81 babies, of which 71 survived weaning.

An earlier experiment measured the quality of the proteins from wheat grown under the two sets of conditions. The wheat was grown at the Rothamstead Research Station where the soil had been fertilized for over one hundred years with either animal manure or inorganic salts. This experiment also failed to show any difference in protein quality – the small difference actually favoured the inorganic salts but was too small to be really true.

There is no evidence at all that organic fertilizers produce more nutritious foods than those grown on commercial farms using various inorganic salts of potassium, phosphate and nitrogen. When used in reasonable amounts, inorganic fertilizers are in no way harmful. The only valid criticism is that when too much is used it can find its way into lakes and ponds, leading to an overgrowth of algae.

HERBICIDES AND INSECTICIDES

Gardeners as well as farmers use an armoury of chemicals to protect their crops from weeds, pests and plant diseases. Their use increases the yield and most modern farming would be uneconomical without them, but are they safe?

When the more modern types of herbicide and insecticide were being developed in the late 1940s, their use was not controlled and many farmers grossly overdosed their crops. Fears were expressed about their persistence in the soil, the effects on wild life and the residues left in food. There was no evidence of harm to human beings, but the possibility that substances such as DDT could accumulate in the body fat gave rise to concern. In fact, it was later shown that after a certain level was reached in the body fat, chemicals were excreted at the same rate as they were ingested. Nevertheless there was some concern arising from the unproven possibility that anyone burning up their body fat during slimming might release this into the bloodstream.

However in 1971 the World Health Organization stated that

the safety record of DDT for man was 'truly remarkable'. At that time about 400,000 tons had been used and whole populations had had their clothes and themselves treated with a powder containing 10 per cent DDT to control malaria and insect infestations – without any ill-effects. It was even added to drinking water to control yellow fever.

Most of these problems have been solved by the development of chemicals which do not persist in the soil and by controlling their use, as well as legislating for levels of residues permitted in foods. While there is no reason to worry about harm, those chemicals left in food do not, of course, do us any good. Hence the appeal of 'health' foods that are claimed – not always correctly – to be entirely free from chemical residues.

The situation is illustrated by a chapter written by Dr. Kenneth Mellanby, then Director of one of Britain's Nature Conservancy Experimental Stations in a book devoted to a return to traditional foods (*Just Consequences, ed. R. Waller, p. 140*). Dr. Mellanby wrote that few of the herbicides or organic phosphorous insecticides in wide use in Britain at the time – 1971 – seemed to be a serious cause of food contamination. Even then, he said, while some of the insecticides accumulated in the body fat, the amount was getting less each year and the amounts in food were decreasing. He pointed out that workers in chemical factories had thirty times as much of these substances in their body fat as the general population without any known ill-effects.

Another example is EDB (ethylene dibromide) used as a fumigant for stored grain and grain machinery and to kill off plant pests in the soil. Laboratory tests in the United States resulted in such panic in the media that the use of EDB was banned in 1984. But it was pointed out by the American Council on Science and Health that two studies of workers engaged in the manufacture of EDB and who had been exposed for sixteen years to 5–10,000 times as much as anyone consuming grain products revealed no evidence of any harm. They also pointed out that an average daily intake of pepper – about 140 milligrams – carries ten to one hundred times the risk of causing cancer as EDB.

The development of more selective chemicals and the greater degree of control exercised today – together with the fact that no evidence of harm has come to light in the intervening years – means that there is little, if any, justification for claims being made for 'health' foods grown without the use of chemicals.

THE RAW FOOD CRAZE

In the history of man, the discovery of fire is relatively recent, only some 40,000 years old. Primitive man was a hunter-gatherer who collected whatever he could find growing in the area as well as hunting animals. Before fire was invented he had no choice but to eat his food raw.

The modern health food addict longs to hark back to the days of the Garden of Eden where man 'must' have eaten what came naturally and 'must' have eaten his food raw. In fact, many raw foods are toxic and only become safe after they have been cooked. Some raw foods contain substances that destroy vitamins, interfere with digestive enzymes or damage the walls of the intestine. Raw meat can be contaminated with bacteria which would be destroyed by cooking; raw fish can contain substances that interfere with vitamin B1 (anti-thiaminases). There have been been very rare cases of a deficiency of biotin (vitamin H) because raw egg white combines with this vitamin and prevents its digestion.

One recent example of poisoning from red kidney beans occurred in Great Britain in 1976 when a party of school-children returned to camp to find that the chicken for their supper had gone bad. There were some red kidney beans soaking ready for the next day, so they ate those raw with salad. Within a few hours the teacher and eight boys were violently sick and two had to go to hospital for treatment. The reaction was caused by natural toxins called haemagglutinins, a group of chemicals which cause red blood cells to clump together (agglutinate) in a test tube. In the bloodstream they would rapidly prove fatal; when taken by mouth they cause nausea, vomiting and diarrhoea within about two hours.

At the same time that the children's accident occurred, there was a trend among health food fans to eat raw kidney beans. Doctors reported 25 outbreaks, affecting about 100 people, to the public health authorities. Reports also spread of red beans still being toxic after cooking in a slow cooker. The amount of toxin was actually increased at low temperatures. As few as four beans were known to make people ill. When the news was broadcast on television, letters from the public revealed at least 100 outbreaks involving 900 people. Since then all packets of dried beans in Great Britain include a health warning on the label telling consumers that the beans should be soaked overnight, the water thrown away and the beans boiled vigorously in fresh water for 10 minutes before any further treatment.

It is surprising that this problem was not recognized until recently because it had, in fact, occurred earlier. The most serious incident, because of the large number of people involved, was during the Berlin airlift in 1948. Among the foods flown in to beat the blockade was a supply of what were called 'flaked beans' – kidney beans that had been incompletely cooked before flaking. Hundreds of people were taken ill after eating them.

This type of poisoning may occur more frequently than is reported. Anyone who has been sick after a meal and recovered a few hours later is not likely to call the doctor. Moreover, if the doctor is called, he may not report the case to a central authority if he diagnoses a mild episode of gastroenteritis. In many countries there is no system of central collection of such data so that the absence of reports on red bean poisoning does not mean that it has not happened.

GRANDMOTHER'S CLAUSE

Health food shops foster the belief that any food or process that is old and traditional is superior to modern food or methods. The sale of 'hand-potted marmalade made in copper vessels' epitomizes this belief. The preference for 'hand-potting' is presumably a reaction against factory machinery although no claims are actually made. The use of copper indicates a return to 'the good old days', before the invention of stainless steel, when copper was the standard material for pans used in jam making. In fact, jam boiled in copper vessels loses all the vitamin C present in the fruit because the vitamin is sensitive to very small traces of copper. Jam made in stainless steel pans retains some of the vitamin C – a couple of ounces of most commercial jam contains just enough to prevent scurvy although blackcurrant jam and marmalade contain more.

A similar attitude was expressed by a spokesman for the Festival of Mind and Body on London Broadcasting Company in 1978 when he said 'if it was good enough years ago it must be good enough now'.

Grandmother's Clause was the nickname given to labelling regulations in Great Britain. The original proposals were intended to make it illegal to use trade names that did not tell the consumer what he was buying. Since names such as Bovril, Gentleman's Relish, Marmite and Ovaltine had been on the market for up to, in some cases, 200 years, it was eventually agreed that products that had been on sale for 30 years or more (and were thus known to the public) could continue without any additional description. New products would require an explanatory name. Even long-established trade names must not be misleading. A lemonade well established in Scotland had to change its name from Iron Brew since it was not a significant dietary source of iron – it is now known as Irn Bru. Someone even suggested that the term Cream Sherry was misleading, but common sense prevailed in this instance.

Apart from the appeal to nostalgia, the fact that a food or process has been in use for centuries would seem to indicate that it does not cause any harm. This may not be true as was explained earlier in the discussion of cabbage and potatoes. When these foods are subjected to the kind of testing applied to food additives, i.e. extracting the chemicals and feeding them in large doses to animals, they fail the test. But unless and until real harm can be proved no government could ban such long-established foods.

Food smoking provides an example of a suspect process where origins have been lost in the mists of time. It may have developed from the custom of suspending meat, fish and cheese curds near the smoke vent in the roof of a cave simply for storage. Much later it was shown that the smoke contains a large number of chemical preservatives and that the heat dries the outer layers of the food, so there is a double preservative action. Nowadays, smoking is used to produce a distinctive flavour and frankfurters, smoked salmon, kippers and smoked eels are common foods. Smoke, however, includes a variety of chemicals such as phenols, tars, aldehydes and ketones – similar chemically to creosote used to preserve wooden fences! Some of these compounds, including benzpyrene, have been identified and shown to cause cancer. Indeed it has been reported from time to time that there is a higher incidence of cancers of the digestive tract among fishermen eating considerable quantities of smoked fish than among the rest of the population, but proof is lacking.

Food scientists have for many years carried out research to reduce or remove the harmful compounds in the smoking process, but the point at issue here is Grandmother's Clause. Unless and until real harm is proven, no government would be willing to ban a traditional food process.

NOVEL FOODS
AND NOVEL PROCESSES

Many suspect foods and processes were introduced long before there was any indication of potential harm and because they have been used for so long without any proof of harm we continue to eat the foods and use the processes. Novel foods and novel processes must undergo the complete range of safety testing and, if the food is likely to replace a traditional food, it must supply the nutrients in similar amounts. The types of novel foods that have been investigated (and some have reached the market) are textured vegetable protein foods made to resemble meat and foods made from yeast and moulds. Novel processes include sterilizing by irradiation, microwave cooking and a process called extrusion cooking.

Some people are harmed by food that is safe for others. For example, about 100 million people, especially in Mediterranean and Middle East countries, cannot eat broad beans. They are born lacking an enzyme in their red blood cells which has no effect unless they eat broad beans, which contain chemicals that break down the red blood cells – a disorder called favism. The beans have no effect on other people. So a food that is safe for one community may not be safe for another. That is why the term 'novel foods' includes not only something quite new like yeast or mould, but also food not previously eaten by people in a particular country. The degree of control of public health and safety exercised now means that strange foods – strange to us although already eaten elsewhere – would still be subjected to testing.

There is no evidence that the novel foods so widely acclaimed in health food shops – carob beans, sesame seeds, buckwheat, oil of evening primrose, extract of green-lipped mussel, garlic oil and a host of herbs – have ever been subjected to such examination. The only reason that food authorities do not demand evidence of safety is that they represent only a small part of the total food eaten – but they may be a large part of the diet of some individuals.

3

COMMODITIES
AND CLAIMS

As stated earlier, it is not the foods sold in health food shops which give rise to criticism, but rather the claims made for them and in particular the extravagant claims made for pills, potions and extracts.

While the foods themselves – such as yoghurt, muesli, honey, wholemeal bread, margarine, cooking oils, nuts and dried fruits – are widely available elsewhere, health food promoters maintain that their products are superior to, as well as 'healthier' than, those on sale in supermarkets. The vast amount of literature available implies that health food products are higher in nutritional content and beneficial to health because they are grown on organically manured soil, with no colours, flavours or processing aids added, and are generally superior to what are termed mass-produced, tasteless, 'manipulated' foods which have been 'tampered' with by large multinational food companies.

There are numerous fallacies here. First, it now seems that in the Western world, on the advice of most nutritionists and medical scientists, we are turning towards foods lower in fats, especially in saturated animal fats, as well as reducing our consumption of cereals. These changes are true for a whole cross-section of the community, not simply health food shoppers. Many of the products we are now buying and which contribute to a healthier diet are being made by the same large-scale producers whose household names are so reviled in health food literature. These manufacturers are producing modified foods in response both to consumer demand and the advice of health educators.

Secondly, health food shops offer few foods which are not available – at lower prices – in supermarkets.

Finally, claims for greater care in food production and preparation, greater regard for hygiene in health food shops and restaurants, greater honesty in labelling the nutritional content and ingredients of the foods they sell, are simply not true. This is evidenced by numerous cases that have reached the law courts. While it is likely that some of these misdemeanours are due to simple error, lack of knowledge or carelessness, it is also apparent that some are due to downright dishonesty. Indeed there may be no more cases brought against health food shops in proportion to their numbers than against ordinary shops, but this is not the point at issue. Health food promoters are claiming superior standards which they do not always fulfil and for which they are, incidentally, charging higher prices.

PROTECTING THE CONSUMER

Great Britain was the first country in the world to have General Pure Food Laws, brought in in 1860. Prior to that legislation related only to certain foodstuffs. There were, as we know from smugglers' tales of old, laws governing the import of brandy which eventually led to regulations concerning the amount of alcohol and sugar in drinks.

As far back as 1266, there was an Act to protect the consumer against short weight in bread and the sale of unsound meat – not that it was effective. Tradesmen's guilds also exercised what controls they could. In the same year there was an Assize of Bread to control its price and quality, with penalities for violation ranging from being put in the pillory to being dragged on hurdles through the streets.

By the beginning of the nineteenth century, the scandalous adulteration of food – often with highly toxic substances – and the general swindling that went on began to be brought to public notice. It was the weekly publication in the *Lancet* of chemical analyses of food that finally led to the Pure Food Act of 1860, which was itself improved and strengthened in 1875.

Over the years, the Act has been extended and steadily improved and is still under continuous scrutiny by consumers' associations and scientific bodies such as the Food Standards Committee and the Food Additives and Contaminants Committee, now combined, assisted by other committees advising on nutritional and safety aspects.

Most other countries now have similar legislation although their procedures may differ. There is a Food and Drug Administration in the United States, a Food and Drug Directorate in Canada and equivalent bodies in nearly every other country as well as advisory bodies in international organizations such as the World Health Organization and the European Economic Community.

In the past the law operated mostly to prevent the harmful adulteration of food and fraud. Over the years, however, the emphasis has changed more towards controlling the composition of made-up manufactured foods (for example the amount of meat or fruit in a pie, the water content of butter and margarine, or the composition of fruit drinks), the information to be given on labels and the maintenance of standards of hygiene.

After Parliament passes legislation in Great Britain, its enforcement is put into the hands of local authorities through their Food Standards and Environmental Health Officers. Anyone with a complaint about hygiene or food adulteration can report it to their local authority which is then bound to investigate the charge.

Cases brought to court are reported in *The British Food Journal* so it is possible for members of the public, as well as scientists and environmental health officers, to keep abreast of developments.

Health food shops, manufacturers and restaurants feature in these court cases as do most of our large supermarkets and food manufacturers. Many infringements of the law may be accidental. Among several million loaves of bread, packets of cereal or bottles of milk a degree of accidental contamination is inevitable, but health food promoters do claim better standards of quality control which they frequently do not meet. Over the past few years, tradesmen selling health foods have been found guilty of selling wheat containing bird droppings and feathers, and sunflower seeds containing rodent droppings; a product labelled 'natural vegetable juice' which contained mould; eggs labelled 'farm fresh' which turned out to be five months old, and 'genuine free-range eggs' which were in fact ordinary battery eggs. One customer who bought a packet of cereal from a health food shop complained the next day that her kitchen sideboard was 'swarming with 30 maggots'. Other cases cite muesli honey cereal, wholewheat spaghetti rings and a special fruit bar which contained moth larvae and eggs.

Such cases are covered by a regulation which finds shopkeepers 'guilty of selling foods which were intended for, but unfit for, human consumption'. Some of these violations were due to shopkeepers buying food, such as sunflower seeds, in bulk in sacks and repacking them on domestic premises (itself an offence). One such shopkeeper offered in his defence the argument that the supplier they used 'had a good name in the health food world'.

One problem arises not merely from carelessness, ignorance and the shopkeeper's own personal standards, but from the inability of a small retailer or manufacturer to exercise adequate quality control. The very criticism which the health food movement offers against large firms is the reason why small companies cannot always do their job properly. Indeed, one small shopkeeper who was found guilty of selling a vitamin C health drink that was actually '96 per cent deficient' in vitamin C, claimed in his defence that his company lacked the facilities to test the vitamin C and had to rely on the supplier (who did, incidentally, accept responsibility and pay a fine). Large manufacturers employ food technologists to check standards of hygiene and quality.

The larger combines in the health food business are as much to blame as any other large company. One health food company was fined for selling an 'exotic honey', further termed 'magic honey', which claimed to contain exotic honeys from various parts of the world when, in fact, it was mainly Australian honey. Another health food combine was found guilty of selling a bottle of vitamin C tablets containing a spider and its web, as well as selling food infested with insect larvae.

Many of the cases of 'ordinary' food that come to court involve minced meat with too much fat, meat pies short of meat and milk containing water. The health food equivalent appears to be a soya-based product (the type called textured vegetable protein, usually intended as a meat substitute) which was deficient in protein. This was, once again, the product of a large-scale manufacturer, not a small shopkeeper. The amount of protein in the cans bore no relation to the claims made on the label – some were 20 per cent, others only 10 per cent of what was stated.

Hygiene in some restaurants and even high-class (or at least highly priced) hotels, is sometimes of a low standard. Some are charged and fined, and occasionally closed down. Health food restaurants have proved no exception. One was described in court as containing rotting food, a dirt-encrusted kitchen and work surfaces, a basement piled with refuse, timber and sacks of decomposing food which was spilling onto the floor. The owner admitted to nineteen charges. One vegetarian restaurant was open less than a year after repeated warnings from health officers. From the start, the owner had been advised on how to comply with regulations, but in court the restaurant was described as having dirty cooking utensils encrusted with grease, worktops which could not be properly cleaned, dirty refrigerators, walls and ceiling in the food store in poor condition, and much more.

One particularly bad example of poor standards of hygiene involved goat's milk. Because there are people allergic to cow's milk, and allergy to goat's milk is relatively rare, it has become renowned as a 'health food'. So it is particularly reprehensible to find a farmer supplying goat's milk guilty of poor hygiene. His products included both cheese and yoghurt. The defence emphasized the severity of the offence by claiming that goat's milk products were intended for people who were ill and could not do without them. The guilt was further compounded by the revealing statement or complaint that the 'visit of the inspector took place before the room was cleaned'.

The Director-General of the Advertising Standards Authority stated in his annual report that the most worrying trend in 1983 was the number of advertisers who were failing to substantiate claims or who were making claims with little or no regard for the evidence to support them. 'Too many of the advertisers concerned appear to begin to dream up a hasty substantiation after the complaint has been made.'

He was not referring specifically to health foods but the remarks clearly apply to them. When, from time to time, the subject of health foods has been discussed at scientific meetings, one regular criticism is that manufacturers and salesmen make claims which they have never even attempted to substantiate. The reply by the health food spokesman is 'why don't you investigate them?' In other words, the health food companies make claims, sell their foods, take their profits and then expect someone else to devote time and money to investigating the truth of the claims.

A rather revealing paragraph appeared in the January and Spring issues of *Health Now* in 1979. It said the manufacture and sale of traditional and safe non-drug herbal remedies, biochemic tissue salts and food supplements which are available through health food shops are subject to all sorts of restrictions and controls. So onerous are these that many remedies have disappeared from the market altogether. The onerous restrictions would appear to be the restriction of unwarranted claims, references to the treatment of diseases which are not allowed and safety to the consumer. It says a lot for the health food trade when the paragraph concludes by saying that 'public choice is under constant attack and is being eroded each day. To this we are totally opposed.'

The facts are that public health authorities are continually improving the law for the protection of the consumer – a procedure to which the health food trade appears to be opposed.

Generally speaking health foods, their claims and the shops which stock them have come in for considerable criticism over the years by health inspectors and environmental health officers. In an article in the *British Food Journal (March/April 1978)* it was stated that figs are used extensively in health foods and these, with barley, seem particularly subject to insect infestation. The same article drew attention to the findings that tonics and restoratives – quinine tonic water was specifically analysed – may be found to contain less of the claimed ingredients than described on the label. In addition: 'specious claims may be made for honey products occasionally invoking biblical exhortations. Kelp tablets, sold for their iodine content, do not state, as the law requires, what the iodine content is.' With reference to vitamin and mineral supplements the article stated damningly: 'when contents are declared they are just as frequently found not to be verified in analysis.' Discussing claims for purity and freedom from chemical additives and pesticides residues: 'the last is difficult to substantiate when the product includes raw fruits and vegetable materials.' As to herbs: 'they are sold with claims that they purify the blood, cleanse it, enrich it, all of which it is almost impracticable to prove either way.'

Indeed, the very terms 'purify', 'cleanse' and 'enrich' are quite meaningless. Blood contains not only a vast number of nutrients on their way to the tissues, but also waste products on their way to the kidneys and lungs for excretion from the body. Does the term 'purify' mean that the products hasten the flow of blood to the kidneys so that it can lose its waste more rapidly? If so, then they are drugs and more likely to be harmful than beneficial. Such claims, if they were taken seriously, would be examined by medical authorities. They are generally regarded by the authorities as 'advertising puff or hype' but seem to be taken seriously by customers.

In a later article in the *British Food Journal (November/December 1983)*, the author went so far as to say: 'A number of these food movements have lunatic fringes which commit terrorist acts to draw attention to themselves ... Some of the reasoning of a number of these cults has no evidence to support them; in fact the contrary is often the case.' The author pointed out that the exaggerated claims made for various food cults may be nothing short of ludicrous: 'Although the literature is abundant many join the movement with inadequate understanding and readily accept far-reaching claims made, some strange, a few stupid and a small number misleading if not downright dishonest.'

It is pertinent to add that a number of deaths have been reported in the United States from cult diets and special so-called slimming foods, an area which will be discussed fully in Chapter 7.

CONTRADICTIONS

Anyone reading the literature supplied by health food promoters – whether free or otherwise – would have great difficulty in separating fact from fantasy. Large health food firms deny the wilder claims, attributing them to 'cowboys', but their own leaflets frequently contradict one another.

Contradictions also occur within the same 'health-promoting' books. For example, Michael Wheatley in *A Way of Living as a Means of Survival – An Encyclopaedia of Natural Health*, advocates a drink made from eggshells dissolved in lemon juice as a high calcium drink (p. 180). Yet later (p. 188) he says that too much calcium can be harmful. After stating that the principal function of bone meal is to supply calcium, he goes on to state that there is little danger in taking too much providing moderation is used (p. 238)!

Mr. Wheatley also contradicts – in this instance correctly – claims for the wonders of lecithin (see the claims by manufacturers under Lecithin, page 85) because he states that it is not strictly a vitamin. In fact, it is not a vitamin at all. He then contradicts himself by saying that it does seem to be essential to health – which would actually qualify it for the title of vitamin. Finally, he says lecithin breaks down fats and holds them in suspension, but also that lecithin helps to put down a layer of fat under the skin.

RIVALRY AND COMPETITION

In one of Rexall's drugstores in California there were, in 1982, 165 vitamin preparations. These included various combinations of A and B, B and C, B1 and B2, with and without iron, copper or caffeine and so on. On the adjacent shelf were 35 additional preparations under Rexall's own brand label.

Every autumn Americans stock up on vitamins, with stores giving special offers – four bottles for the price of three, discounts, reduced prices for bulk purchases and one cent for a second bottle (one bottle cost $3.99 and for $4 you could get an extra bottle). What might well be described as the best-fed nation in the world has been led by the health food movement to believe that it will go short of nutrients unless tablets, capsules, pills and powders of vitamins, minerals and various food extracts are added to an already excessive diet.

On a visit to New York I was in a gigantic self-service restaurant in Times Square. A man sat next to me with a tray containing enough food to last a normal person half a week – and a glass of milk. When asked why he drank the milk, he replied, 'That is for my nutrition.' So brainwashed is the American public that food and nutrition are regarded as separate concerns.

So writes the 'superior' Englishman, but are we any better? Close scrutiny of the numerous health magazines – and new ones are appearing every few months – reveals a plethora of vitamins, minerals, Oriental extracts, pills and potions, each extolled by its manufacturer and denigrated by its rivals.

You can buy vitamin E in small, medium, large and extra large doses, vitamins of the B complex varying from three ingredients to as many as 50, supplemented with all sorts of extracts that make them 'more available', or at least 'superior' to those of their rivals. Add to all these varieties the numerous manufacturers selling identical products under different trade names and you will probably conclude that the British public – and the Australian, German and Swiss to name but a few – are just as gullible as the Americans.

ARE THEY ANY GOOD?

It is now a truism that the greater the lie, the more likely it is to be believed. According to the health food literature, ALL – and they really say all – the ills of modern industrialized society are due to a bad diet.

This can be remedied, so the authors and advertisers tell us, by taking their natural, or organically grown, wholefood products, or vitamin supplements, 'chelated minerals', enzyme preparations or snake medicine.

In fact, there is hardly a grain of truth behind most of these claims. Certainly we can improve our diet, certainly many people eat relatively poorly, but to suggest that everyone will gain youth, vitality, sexual vigour, freedom from disease and all the other claims that are made by one manufacturer or another strains the credulity. There are enough people who do believe these claims, however, to make continued sales worthwhile.

Some claims are far-fetched, some merely wildly extravagant, but some are sufficiently untrue to be labelled dishonest. They certainly break the law, as evidenced by the court cases that crop up from time to time.

The consumer magazine *Which?*, in its *June 1978* issue, reported many inaccuracies. For example, they found then that Alfonal margarine had just the same list of ingredients as most other brands of soft margarine – emulsifiers, colours and flavours. Half of the twenty samples of dried fruit examined had been treated with sulphur dioxide, a preservative, and mineral oil, to keep them sticky.

The point was made that soya protein granules and chunks are made by a highly sophisticated factory process: by

54

extracting the oil from the soya bean, heating then treating with pressure or dissolving and spinning to make fibres. Finally vitamins and minerals are added. Similar highly processed foods include vegetarian pâtés, sausages and cold meat substitutes.

The article concluded that: 'You can't be sure that all the foods in "health food" shops match up to "health" food principles' – principles that the manufacturers have said they support, as described on page 89.

Some manufacturers actually admit that they have no evidence to support the claims they make. In *Natural Choice No. 10*, a leaflet published by the health food chain Holland and Barrett describing the value of herbal remedies, it is stated: 'claims that can be made for a herbal remedy are often restricted by the lack of hospital trial proof, the only kind that is now officially accepted.' Concerning garlic, the leaflet states: 'such useful relaying of information [i.e. people who say it does them good] carries no weight with the scientific community as proof.' Yet salesmen do make claims and sell products without real evidence of their value.

Finally, let me quote from a speech made by Hilde Bruch of Baylor College of Medicine, Houston, Texas at a meeting of the Swedish Nutrition Foundation and published on the general subject *Food Cultism and Nutrition Quackery*.

'There is no doubt that many . . . promoters are undisguised frauds and swindlers who knowingly sell worthless nostrums to a duped clientele and are bent on commercial exploitation of the frightened and helpless.

'Others are crackpots, convinced of the merits of their discoveries and insights, who want to make converts on their road to health and salvation.'

Some of the products on sale are worth examining from the point of view of the claims made for them and what they really are.

ACID AND ALKALI

There is a great deal of misunderstanding about acid and alkali where food is concerned, not that it matters because the body has an enormous capacity to deal with vinegar (even cider vinegar), lemon juice or pickled onions, which are strongly acid, as well as baking powder or bicarbonate which are strongly alkaline.

Stomach acidity is the production of too much gastric acid and has nothing to do with the quantity of acid or alkaline foods we eat. The confusion is due to the difference between foods which taste acid and foods which leave an acid residue after their other components have been metabolized in the body. For example, orange juice contains citric acid and sodium citrate – and some oranges taste very acid. In the body, the citric acid and the citrate part of the sodium citrate are burned off to provide energy (with carbon dioxide and water being the waste products). The citric acid is burned off completely but the sodium citrate leaves the sodium behind, and this is alkaline. So acid-tasting orange juice actually leaves an alkaline residue behind.

Meat, fish, poultry, eggs, cheese, cereals and certain nuts leave an acid residue after the rest has been burned off; most fruit, vegetables and other nuts leave an alkaline residue. None of this matters, however, because the body deals very effectively with both. The blood, despite claims that cider vinegar does magic things in the bloodstream, is maintained very closely at a stage just on the alkaline side of exact neutrality. Acidity and alkalinity are measured by a unit called pH which runs from zero – extremely strong acid – to 14 – strong caustic soda. Both are potent enough to burn holes in a carpet. pH 7 is exact neutrality, neither acid nor alkaline. Fruit juices with a pH below 4 taste very sour and below 3 are quite unpalatable. Most foods have a pH between 5 and 8.

The pH of blood is kept very constant, between 7.35 and 7.45, and the body is adept at keeping our blood at just the right level. Any extra acid or alkali that is left after our food has been metabolized is excreted in the urine. The pH of urine can vary quite normally between 4.8 and 8.0 without causing any harm. So advice from health food enthusiasts selling acid or alkaline food supplements is quite incorrect.

ALOE VERA

Aloe vera is a plant claimed to be 'one of nature's botanical wonders, retaining a respected place in medicine through the ages. The Romans, Greeks, Arabs, Indians and Chinese used it both medicinally and cosmetically.' It is still advertised, without any justification, as being suitable for both these widespread purposes.

The juice of the plant is made up of about 25 per cent sugars – principally glucose and mannose, with a small amount of protein, fat, some vitamins and minerals – as indeed are all plant juices, not excluding grass juice. Taken by mouth, the dried latex is a severe cathartic – a purgative – but no harm has been reported. Nor has any benefit been reported for its claimed virtues.

Beauticians have a range of products containing aloe vera – shampoos, cleansing lotions, moisturizers, in juice, jelly and lotion form. It is also an ingredient in eye make-up remover, epidermic face cream, lifting gell, nail grower and bio-B deep cleanser.

It is claimed as a treatment for radiation burns, brown skin spots, psoriasis, varicose veins, eczematous rashes, and skin cancer. When taken orally, it is said to be good for arthritis, and is advocated as a food supplement. The claims even go so far as to say that it enhances cell regeneration, can be used as a cosmetic facelift, producing a youthful look by tightening the skin while the cells are being built, blocks out sunburning rays, reduces scarring and adds lustre to the hair.

No wonder it is a botanical wonder – you can use it inside and out!

CIDER VINEGAR

Some of the most far-fetched, improbable and dishonest

claims of all are made for cider vinegar. Its magical properties were popularized by an American doctor who found that people in the state of Vermont lived an abnormally long time (this doubtful claim is discussed in full on page 126). He also found that these people drank cider vinegar – which proved conclusively to him that cider vinegar lengthens the lifespan. Among his other 'findings' was that, when taken by pregnant women, their babies were born with full heads of hair.

Of course the manufacturers cashed in and described cider vinegar as: 'the perfect cleanser of the body acting on the liver and disposing of poisons'. It is also claimed to be 'a medicine for the overweight because it improves metabolism and so deals with excess fat'. It is said to prevent obesity by helping the 'natural assimilation of carbohydrates'. Such statements are both unjustified and quite untrue.

Vinegar is a solution of acetic acid, dilute enough to put on French fries or salad as a dressing. It comes in three varieties.

Unbrewed vinegar is a simple solution of acetic acid, with little flavour apart from its acidity.

Then there is brewed vinegar which is made by a fermentation process like wine but finishes up as acetic acid instead of alcohol. Just as with wine, the fermentation produces a number of substances in small amounts that give a 'bouquet' and hence a better flavour than simple acetic acid.

Finally, there is wine or cider vinegar. This is wine or cider that has re-fermented – as home winemakers sometimes find to their dismay – changing the alcohol to acetic acid. All the pleasant flavours of the wine or cider remain, so that the resulting vinegar has the best flavour.

Chemically and nutritionally wine and cider vinegar are both a 4.8 per cent solution of acetic acid with no protein, fat or vitamins and only minute traces of minerals. Claims that cider vinegar's marvellous properties are due to its high potassium content are untrue. Apples themselves contain only 120 mg of potassium in 100 g – and some cider vinegar preparations contain only 20 mg of cider vinegar – which would, even if they were pure apple juice, supply only 0.02 mg of potassium. Compare this with 150 mg of potassium in 100 g of white flour or 450 mg in the same amount of wholemeal flour and 350 mg in 100 g of meat, chicken, fruit or vegetables. Even one raisin at 860 mg of potassium per 100 g will provide more than most of these cider vinegar preparations.

Nonetheless, cider vinegar is advertised as a gargle or drink to relieve laryngitis, coughs, asthma, arthritis and rheumatic complaints. It is claimed to benefit bleeding haemorrhoids, chronic headaches, dizziness, high blood pressure, nose bleeding, sore throats and pyelitis, as well as being a 'recommended treatment' for gout and intestinal disorders.

According to Balfour and Allen's book, *The A to Z of Health Food Terms*, apple cider is a valuable food for rebuilding the body. But acetic acid provides just 2 Calories to the gram and no protein so you could not build much body with that. The same book also states that cider vinegar helps to control the bacteria in the intestine. This cannot be true because cider vinegar is absorbed from the intestine before it reaches the part where the bacteria live. The authors also claim that it stops calcium being deposited in the tissues when the blood becomes too alkaline, but if your blood became too alkaline you would be dead and beyond worrying about calcium. In fact, all statements about acetic acid entering the blood are untrue because acetic acid as such does not enter the blood – it is neutralized by the alkaline digestive juices long before that. Balfour and Allen even claim that cider vinegar tenderizes the tissues – presumably useful for a cannibal but hardly an advantage otherwise and not true anyway.

Advertisers maintain that two teaspoons of cider vinegar will take an inch off the waistline in two months, a second inch in the next two months, and a third inch by the end of the fifth month. This is said – quite incorrectly – to be due to the effect of the vinegar in eliminating fat from the body instead of allowing it to be stored. An Australian claim (*Healthy Life News of Australia, January 1984*) even says that it breaks up fat globules in the bloodstream.

In 1982 a complaint against an advertisement by the Health and Dietary Food Store which had advertised that a course of Cidersin B capsules would disperse unwanted fat, was upheld by the Advertising Standards Authority.

The final claim in this list is the only one that is correct – cider vinegar will remove calcium scale from the kettle!

DNA

DNA and RNA are abbreviations for Deoxyribonucleic acid and ribonucleic acid. Put simply, they are both part of all living cells and control the basis of heredity and cell multiplication. They came to public knowledge when the principal research workers involved won the Nobel Prize and explained their work in a book called *The Double Helix*.

They are quite unnecessary in the diet because the body makes all it needs. Furthermore, it is dangerous to consume too much. This has become an important public health problem over the past 20 or 30 years with the development of yeasts, algae, moulds and even bacteria as food. These small cells, often grouped together as so-called 'single-cell proteins', contain a much larger proportion of their cells as the nucleus and so a much greater proportion of these nucleic acids – DNA and RNA. When consumed, DNA and RNA finish up as uric acid, and if the level rises too high in the blood can cause problems. Blood normally contains about 1–5 mg per 100 ml, increased to 8–15 mg in gout. People with kidney disorders (renal insufficiency) cannot dispose of the uric acid, causing a rise to harmful levels in the blood and the suffering of gout.

Yet we find health food shops selling DNA and RNA, distributing free leaflets making claims for it, and articles in books and magazines recommending it as a 'natural dietary aid for the genetic building material'. An advertisement for Cantara says that it contains 450 g of 'pure, natural DNA' and that as one gets older the body does not seem to be able to make enough RNA from food. It is recommended for younger people 'who wish to see if their faculties can be tuned further with this natural concentrate' (another nonsensical use of the term natural).

One product consisting of RNA and DNA claimed to halt,

slow down and reverse the aging process. The leaflet claimed that people aged from thirty to fifty appeared to lose five to ten years of age after three months of treatment. 'In older patients afflicted with coronary heart disease and congestive heart failure, the heart function was clearly improved. An increase in mental acuity was observed, particularly in the improvement of memory.' The leaflet even goes so far as to say, incorrectly, that there are no contra-indications for such a product.

In fact, the potential dangers are so great that the World Health Organization and the Food and Agriculture Organization have spent a great deal of time over the past twenty years in developing methods of reducing the levels of DNA and RNA in yeasts and algae. A new food made from a mould preparation was not permitted by the health authorities in Great Britain until the RNA had been reduced to a quarter of the level naturally present. The manufacturers were fully aware of the dangers and themselves carried out research to fulfil this demand.

ENZYMES

Enzymes are chemical agents made of protein that carry out specific functions in the body. There are thousands of them and their functions range from digesting food (with different enzymes for fats, carbohydrates and proteins) and synthesizing the tissues of our body to burning up fats, carbohydrates and proteins to supply us with energy.

The body makes all the enzymes we need, even when the diet is as poor as it is in some developing countries, so taking extra is useless. One reason for this is that the enzymes offered for sale are not human, but have been extracted by chemical processes from plant and animal tissues. Another reason is that they are inactivated in the stomach because the acid coagulates the protein (just as when an egg is boiled) and they are then simply digested and used like any other protein we eat.

The *Which?* survey of *June 1978* says that wholefood

enthusiasts stress that cooking can destroy the enzymes in our food (true) and continues 'don't worry, your body makes its own'. So all the pills and tablets that contain what are usually described as 'valuable enzymes and biocatalysts' are no more valuable or useful to us than the protein in a slice of bread.

GARLIC

Garlic has been used medicinally for centuries. The Ancient Egyptians believed that it held the secret of youth. In the Middle Ages, people used to wrap garlic or onions in a piece of cloth and tie it around their necks to keep colds at bay. The Roman historian, Pliny, recommended garlic for the treatment of madness but his claims lose credence when you learn that he also considered it to be an aphrodisiac.

Nearly 2000 years later garlic is claimed by its promoters to be the supreme health food supplement and the 'evidence' offered is that, apart from Pliny, the Egyptians, Babylonians and the Greeks, 'all of whom are fathers of modern medicine,' thought very highly of it. One typical advertisement reads:

'So many common ailments that we have to contend with – such as catarrh, bronchial troubles, blood disorders, rheumatism and skin complaints for example – are due to impurities and toxins which have accumulated in the system because the bloodstream has been unable to eliminate them. These poisons may prevent the efficient working of vital organs and sooner or later sow the seeds of serious ill-health. Nature provides a supreme internal antiseptic in garlic and garlic should be taken regularly, just by itself, as a normal addition to the daily intake of food.'

In fact, garlic is one of the herbal remedies that may have beneficial effects, if not quite the extravagant cure-all claims which are made for it. It has been shown experimentally to reduce the levels of blood cholesterol in rabbits and since high levels of blood cholesterol are 'risk factors' in coronary heart disease, this may be beneficial to human beings. There is no sound evidence to prove that lowering the levels of blood cholesterol will actually save anyone from a heart attack, but any reduction of the numerous risk factors might be helpful. The doses that have been used experimentally in rats are far greater, proportionately, than those in the garlic capsules offered for sale. Apart from this, however, there is no evidence that, as Michael Wheatley claims, garlic is 'nature's antibiotic, improves digestion and assimiliation, or prevents pneumonia and typhus' (*A Way of Living as a Means of Survival – An Encyclopaedia of Natural Health*). It may be true that it was used in the Middle Ages against the Plague (not very effectively it would seem) and the advertisers are careful not to break the law when they say 'it has been used to treat cancer'. Statements such as this last which cruelly raise unjustified hopes are particularly regrettable.

GINSENG

Ginseng is the 'health food' par excellence and is sold in the form of powders, teas, tablets and extracts. Five to six million Americans take ginseng and it is one of South Korea's major exports. Its 5000-year history is of great help to health food promoters.

Ginseng is a small shrub that needs to grow for six to seven years before its roots are large enough to harvest. This is used as a selling point on the grounds that the plant takes so many minerals and valuable trace elements from the ground that the soil needs ten years to recover, and that the plant, therefore, must be far richer than any other in these nutrients. No evidence is offered in support of this claim.

There are several rival preparations on the market and the *Chinese Materia Medica* itself explained (long before health food shops were ever thought of) that there are five true varieties and several fraudulent ones. Of the five genuine varieties, one is used for pulmonary disease, one acts on the spleen, kidney, liver and heart and is a restorative of bodily vigour, another, Jin-shen, is a restorative of the yang principle (see Macrobiotics, page 172), while the variety Sha-shen restores the yin. Jan-shen was the 'best' variety, reserved for the Chinese Royal Family being, according to the 1911 edition of the translation of the book, 'worth 250 times its weight of silver'. A few hundred years ago the Koreans, obviously foreseeing a brilliant future, cultivated the crop for ordinary folk and this is now the principal source.

The claims made in books and leaflets advertising ginseng reflect the Chinese writings of *Sin-Nung Pen T'sao Ching* of 2000 years ago. 'It quiets the animal spirit, establishes the soul, allays the fears, expels the evil effluvia, invigorates the body, opens up the heart and benefits the understanding.'

Modern literature offers users a long, healthy and happy life with this 'natural' tonic that restores, maintains and builds up the whole system. 'While no direct claims can be made that ginseng ensures longevity' the leaflets do suggest that this belief clearly springs from the contribution ginseng makes to our general well-being.

It is said to be so good that the Vietcong rushed into battle against the Americans armed with ginseng. It is used in Russia, so the literature says, in the treatment of depression and lack of vitality; in Bermuda to overcome tiredness and loss of memory; by telephone operators to keep themselves alert and efficient. It is claimed to have the remarkable properties of being able to normalize both high and low blood pressure. It is both a sedative and a stimulant. These apparently contradictory properties are 'explained' by claims that the body adapts the plant to suit itself. A new word – 'adaptogen' – was coined to describe the mystical – and as yet undiscovered – chemicals in the root.

In fact, the scientific evidence offered by the ancient Chinese was not all that convincing. Consider the test described in the *Chinese Pharmacopoeia* for 'true' ginseng. 'Two people walk together, one with a piece of the true drug in his mouth – after 3 to 5 li (a mere 1 to 2 miles) the one without the ginseng is out of breath, the other does not feel tired.'

The rival products available offer obvious contradictions to one another but there are also contradictions within the same products. One leaflet, for example, says the whole root should be used rather than the extract, yet the same firm sells ginseng tea. Another firm says that you should boil or steam the root for five to six hours and then drink the extract.

The Russian version is not technically ginseng at all, but is claimed to be superior. It is not Panax, the botanical name for ginseng of various species, but Eleutherococcus. The seed is said to have been sent from Manchuria to St. Petersburg in 1853 but research started only in the 1950s by Professor Brekham at the Insitute of Biologically Active Substances in Vladivostok. He showed it to be superior to ginseng because 'It brings bodily functions back to normal no matter what the nature of the disorder.' This is all due to 'adaptogens'. It is also said to act on cancer cells by 'weakening their toxic effect'. So it comes as no surprise to read that the Russian government supplies it to factory workers and finds that it increases work output by reducing the incidence of catarrh and influenza.

WHAT IS IT?

Ginseng has been subjected to considerable laboratory investigation since the 1950s, partly because of these claims, and partly to ascertain whether its sale over the counter is safe. Like all biological materials it contains a large number of chemicals, including thirteen of a group of chemicals that produce a soapy solution with water, saponins. In the Japanese literature they are called 'ginsenosides', and in the Russian literature 'panaxosides'. Saponins are found in a wide variety of plants and their foaming properties have been used in fire extinguishers and foamy drinks.

Many tests have been carried out on experimental animals but the results are controversial. When mice were subjected to exhaustive exercise by making them swim for life, find their way out of a maze or climb a pole, they were able to continue longer when given ginseng. Such findings serve as the basis for the health, strength and vigour claims and, indeed, athletes hopefully try the products and are used in advertising campaigns.

Some of the confusion arises from contradictory results coming from the same laboratory. In the *Japanese Journal of*

Pharmacology of 1977, a paper from the University of Tokyo found that ginseng depressed the central nervous system in three rats and stimulated it in two rats (depression of the central nervous system is the same effect as that produced by tranquillizers). The question of whether to eat or drink the various ginseng preparations on the market is made even more difficult to answer when we find that these Japanese experimenters injected the materials into the rats.

IS IT SAFE?

Generally, results of laboratory trials indicate that ginseng is safe but there are several disturbing reports. A letter published in the *British Medical Journal* in 1978 reported that an elderly woman developed swollen tender breasts (mastalgia) with diffuse nodules after taking ginseng powder for three weeks – despite experiencing a feeling of well-being. The symptoms disappeared when she stopped taking ginseng, but appeared twice more when she re-started. Doctors suggested that the effect might be due to hormones present in the product.

This was followed by a letter from the Netherlands Department of Health and the Environment (*British Medical Journal, 17 June 1978*) pointing out that ginseng not only contained the female sex hormones – oestrone, oestradiol and oestriol – but other substances as well, one of which may interfere with the regulation of diabetes and another which was chemically related to digitoxin and could, in theory, cause problems in patients already taking certain drugs for heart conditions.

A paper in the *Journal of the American Medical Association* in 1979 commented on what was called Ginseng Abuse Syndrome. Doses as little as 3 g have been reported to cause insomnia, nervousness, confusion, 'feelings of depersonalization' and depression as well as skin eruptions, oedema and diarrhoea.

Finally there is the problem of finding out just what you are buying. The various preparations on sale are not standardized – some are extracts which inevitably differ, others are claimed to be the whole, powdered root, and there are different varieties of the plant itself. Furthermore, in a review in the *Pharmaceutical Journal (11 February 1984, p. 161)* it is reported that a study in the United States showed that seven out of twenty-four samples purchased did not contain any ginseng at all. Other samples had only one fifth of the amount that is normally present in the root. The reviewer said of these and other products that 'some herbal preparations are not adequately controlled analytically and can be called "cowboy" preparations.'

The Daily Mail (2 October 1979) reported that sales of ginseng in Britain amounted to £3 million a year. Prices ranged from £5.98 for a 100 g jar of ginseng tea, to the 'highest quality', 'whole root of heaven' at £179.40. It went on to quote a former president of the British Institute of Medical Herbalists on eight products that were on sale, some with added pollen and so-called vitamin F or vitamin E, and varieties of straight ginseng. His comments included: 'Claims made for pollen and vitamin E are based on very unclear evidence and the ginseng is present in amounts too small to do any good.' Regarding a ginseng shampoo, he said: 'Won't do you any harm – the word "rejuvenating" is very misleading.' With regard to one product which included mention of a dose on the label, he said: 'This would then be classed as a medicine ... the ingredients must all be stated on the box.' They were not.

Since ginseng is a big money spinner, it is naturally the subject of intense rivalry between manufacturers. Those who sell Panax deny that Russian ginseng is the real thing and those who sell the Russian version claim that it combines the latest Russian ideas in nutrition. Russian sportsmen and astronauts are given doses. But just in case the customer wants it, the same firm also sells Oriental ginseng with or without added vitamins, and/or vitamin B6 and/or zinc and/or poly-unsaturated fatty acids.

THE GREEN-LIPPED MUSSEL

This is a fair description of the sea creature Perna canaliculata. The extracts, variously known as seatone and oceantone, have been widely promoted, as have so many other cures, for the treatment of rheumatic disorders. It contains some amino acids, fat, carbohydrate and mineral salts. With the publicity it received, it was tried out by many medical scientists but reports in 1978, 1980 and 1981 all showed it to have no effect whatsoever. Yet it is still offered for sale in health food shops for the treatment of rheumatism.

HERBAL REMEDIES

Herbal medicine is one of the areas of alternative medicine that has never been properly evaluated by conventional scientists. In the hands of trained medical herbalists it would appear to be at least safe and possibly effective in treating certain specified disorders. The problem arises from over the counter sales of herbal remedies. The market in Great Britain, currently worth £20 million a year, appears to be booming, judging from the number of shops of all kinds entering the business.

The attraction of these 'remedies' is obvious. How the names trip off the tongue – maidenhair and pennyroyal, star grass, sweetflag, colt's foot, devil's claw, beggar's blanket and witches' candle, wake-robin, deer's tongue, snakeroot and Lizzie run-in-the-hedge.

The very fact that they have been used over the centuries is offered as proof that 'they must be good for us'. Indeed, much of the current literature is based on the writings of the Chinese scientist, Li Si Zhen, of 1550 and of Nicholas Culpeper (1616–54). Herbalists in Great Britain were given a charter from King Henry VIII in 1542.

WHAT ARE THEY?
Technically herbs are described as low-growing, seasonal

plants. Some are sources of well-known poisons – hemlock, strychnine and cyanide. Others are the source of medicines – such as quinine from tree bark, aspirin from willow bark and digitalis from foxgloves – although these are now synthesized in the laboratory.

While herbs may be of value in the hands of trained medical herbalists the indiscriminate sale of dried roots, leaves, stems, flower petals and extracts made from them has led to positive harm. There are some 2600 herbal preparations available – some have been tested for safety and for their curative effect but many have not.

WHAT IS CLAIMED?

A review of herbal remedies in the *Pharmaceutical Journal (14 January 1984, p. 41)* states that therapeutic claims in many instances have not been validated The statements that are made claim cures for every ill known to mankind. An Australian 'health' leaflet claims that chickweed suppresses the appetite and so is good for slimmers, that hawthorn berries remove fatty deposits like cellulite, that liquorice counters 'that run-down feeling that slimmers often go through', that sarsaparilla purifies the blood – a common but meaningless term beloved of health food salesmen – and that parsley improves the circulation – again, meaningless.

The general claim, as offered in the definition of herbs in *The A to Z of Health Food Terms* (Balfour and Allen), is that the treatment is 'safe, non-toxic and long-term in action'.

The evidence that herbal treatment is not always 'safe and non-toxic' is discussed below. The suggestion that it is 'long-term in action' seems to suggest that we must continue buying the product even if we do not feel any good effects. No one claims that herbal remedies are effective in emergencies, but rather that they take weeks to act. This, it is said, is because they help to build up the body's own natural defences against disease. But there is no evidence that this is true. Many people do get better whatever their treatment – doctors often admit that the sheet and the mattress are the best cures. So doing nothing, or going to bed, or just waiting – and perhaps taking a herbal remedy at the same time – may effect a cure.

Herbs are good for everything it would seem. A treatment that glories in the name of aromatotherapy – a technique straddling conventional beauty treatments and medicine – claims that essential oils distilled from plants and herbs can penetrate the bloodstream and reach far into vital organs such as the kidney and liver to give great psychological benefits by their smell. Various oils have different properties – diuretic, antiseptic and restorative. The beauty treatment includes taking kelp and verbena tea. Treatments cost £20, including an initial consultation and massage, with essential oils at £6 a phial. A course of ten treatments costs £144.

ARE THEY REALLY SAFE?

The potential harm of natural herbal remedies was examined in an editorial in the *British Medical Journal (3 March 1979)*. In discussing self-medication with health foods and herbal medicines, it was stated that: '... not all the agents they use are benign and some can cause serious injury and even death. Neither patient nor doctor may be aware of their constituents, let alone the possible toxicity of substances taken as medicines.'

Various herbal remedies – ragwort and herbal teas were specifically mentioned – contain alkaloids which can cause severe liver damage. Reports of this from five countries were referred to.

After mentioning poisonous plants that caused deaths in the Far East, the author stated that some of the medicinal preparations sold over the counter in Britain may also prove to have serious toxic effects. The article concludes by saying: 'Manufacturers should be obliged to give factual descriptions of these (the exact constituents), which would help to dispel the mystique that all too often surrounds "fringe" medicines.'

The *British Medical Journal* reprinted a note from the United States of a young woman who complained of blurred vision, dry mouth, hallucinations and retention of urine after drinking burdock tea bought from a health food shop *(Journal of American Medical Association, 1978, 239, p. 2157).* The report said: 'Surprisingly there have been no previous reports of toxic effects.' Perhaps they have occurred but have not been reported because no one would expect a plant like burdock to be harmful.

In the journal *Chemistry and Industry (6 November 1982)* the product manager of Potter's of Wigan, the largest specialist suppliers of herbal goods, was reported as saying at a meeting of the Pharmaceutical Society of Great Britain that some products are wrongly labelled and of questionable quality. He added that provided that they are not advertised directly as cures for particular ailments there is little or no legal control.

They are, however, extensively advertised in leaflets distributed by health food shops and in articles written in 'health' magazines as being beneficial for virtually every ill known to man. Moreover manufacturers are able to market remedies with packaging that suggests that the contents are drugs while their sale is actually covered only by food quality regulations. As mentioned in Chapter 1, the dangers in many 'health' remedies lie not only in their toxins but in the fact that advertisments lead to self-medication which may dangerously delay proper medical attention.

A commentary in the *Journal of the American Medical Association (7 November 1980, p. 2053)* summarized the position thus: 'My patient explained – first you identify your complaint or the area you want to work on. Then you go to a chart in a natural food store to see which herb combination is recommended. "Since I have high blood pressure, I found this listing on my chart."' The herbs cited included cayenne, parsley, ginger root, golden seal root, garlic and Siberian ginseng. Their physiological action was said to promote overall blood circulation and tended to normalize high and low blood pressure. Cholesterol build-up in the blood vessels could also be reduced. When the doctor asked for evidence he was told: 'People swear by these herbs. Besides, herbs have been used in folk medicine for millennia. What better proof can there be?' He pointed out that leeches were used for centuries but that didn't prove their value, and 'the patient developed a far-away look'. 'I am assaulting something that he is unwilling to question.'

An editorial comment in a similar vein in the *Journal of the American Medical Association (1980, p. 2091)* stated that: 'Nature worship is still a force to be reckoned with.' This was in response to an article by a doctor whose patient persisted in believing in the virtues of herbal medicines. In the herb book recommended to him by his patient, the doctor read that fenugreek tea was preferable to antacid tablets for indigestion sufferers 'because it neutralizes stomach acid safely and effectively'. The doctor tested out the antacid properties and found no such effect. In the same book, he found a 'quotation' from a scientist from the U.S. National Cancer Institute stating that the violet plant damages the cancer in a cancerous mouse. The doctor wrote to the author who had been quoted and he replied that this was not true. Continuing his research into natural cures, the doctor became concerned when he read that sage tea and capsicum gargle were being recommended for quinsy. He pointed out the risk of delaying medical treatment for such a potentially fatal disease.

SOME PLANTS AND THEIR EFFECTS

Celery
The fact that a plant grows 'in nature' does not necessarily make it either good for us, or safe. Celery is an attractive food despite its low level of nutrients, but even that can cause problems.

A group of chemicals called psoralenes are found in plants in amounts of 1 part in a million (100 micrograms in 100 g). These are found in celery and when the plant is diseased it produces 100 times as much in order to increase its defences. Celery pickers and handlers commonly develop skin rashes on their arms when exposed to diseased celery *(Ames, Science, September 1983, p. 1256)*.

72

Comfrey

This plant, a member of the borage family, is lauded as having powers in mending fractures and curing asthma, digestive disorders, boils, eczema and ulcers. Whether these claims are true is open to doubt, not dispelled by saying that it was used by the ancient Greeks and Romans 'as a herb of gladness and courage' nor by the knowledge that growing comfrey is a big business in Japan (*Holland and Barrett Express, January/February 1983*). The article says that if only a percentage of all the cures attributed to comfrey were successful, then it would indeed be an amazing plant, a statement that suggests that the writer does not really believe it. The article continues by claiming that the plant is rich in phosphorus, and vitamins A, B and C – as usual without any supporting evidence. It is very doubtful indeed whether comfrey is any 'richer' in these substances than any other leafy vegetable.

One claim that was made – and for some years accepted – about comfrey was that it was one of the very few plant sources of vitamin B12, and therefore a boon to vegans. Unfortunately this is not true (*Martindale, The Extra Pharmacopoeia*). The author of the article in the *Holland and Barrett Express* is not only unaware of this, but even goes so far as to explain exactly why comfrey contains B12 – because 'its roots penetrate to 10 feet enabling it to extract vitamin B12 in particular from the subsoil.' It is not clear why short roots do not do the same, since soil bacteria produce vitamin B12 even in topsoil.

Apart from its lack of nutritional and medicinal benefits, comfrey has been shown to be toxic. It can cause cancer in the liver of rats and contains the toxic substances called pyrrolizidine alkaloids, especially in the small, young leaves early in its growing season.

Comfrey may be safer applied externally, since it contains 0.7 per cent of a substance called allantoin, which was formerly applied to wounds. Allantoin itself is sold in health food stores in order, it is claimed, to stimulate tissue formation and the healing of wounds. Whatever it may do when applied to the outside of the body, it is useless when taken orally as it is actually a waste product excreted in small amounts in human urine.

Mistletoe

The December 1982 *Lancet* carried an editorial entitled 'Baleful Mistletoe'. This plant has a long history. It was venerated by the Druids and, even earlier, Loki, the Norse god of evil, killed Balder, the sun god, with an arrow made from mistletoe. This clearly makes it a good candidate for a 'health food'. The editorial said:

> *'It is not only used by witch doctors in the Third World; until 1978 Felsol, a prescription drug containing mistletoe extract, was marketed in Britain for the treatment of asthma and in Portsmouth a herbalist is reported to sell 30,000 mistletoe-containing pills every week. Some 150 mistletoe-containing products are available in Britain.'*

The article went on to say that the berries contain three classes of potentially toxic compounds – alkaloids, viscotoxins and lectins – and that the ingestion of the berries in large amounts causes gastroenteritis.

In spite of such dangers, one mistletoe preparation on the market claimed to have 'no known side-effects, incompatibilities or risks when following directions'.

Sassafras

Sassafras tea was banned by the U.S. Food and Drug Administration in 1976 because the safrole that it contains caused liver cancer in rats.

Verbena

This is marketed as a tisane – a herbal extract as a drink – free from caffeine and tannin. Yet in *The A to Z of Health Food Terms*, Balfour and Allen claim that verbena contains a particular kind of tannic acid which acts as a nerve tonic and antispasmodic remedy, especially in the case of epilepsy.

WHY ARE THEY NOT STOPPED?

The large number of herbal preparations on the market must include the good, the bad and the indifferent. Specialists in herbal treatment say that training in the subject takes several years. As regards inaccurate and misleading claims and potentially harmful effects, herbs are in the same category as so many other 'health foods'. Some manufacturers sincerely believe in them – and they may well be right – but others are simply bending and twisting the law to make money from a gullible and often suffering public. A review in the *Pharmaceutical Journal (14 January 1984, p. 41)* listed some of the toxic substances found in plants and stated that herbs should be treated as medicines rather than ordinary commodities. Ill health, injury and even deaths have resulted from over the counter purchase of these apparently harmless substances.

The public is not completely powerless, however. In addition to being very careful about buying such preparations, misleading and incorrect claims can be stopped by drawing them to the attention of the Advertising Standards Authority and the local trading standards officer. From time to time complaints are made and action is taken. For example, an advertisement for Quiet Life Tablets claimed that they were free from drugs and made from natural herbs with added B vitamins. In fact, the product contained plant alkaloids, which are drugs, and a complaint laid against the manufacturer was upheld by the Advertising Standards Authority *(ASA Case Report 102)*. Similarly claims for the Oriental Quikslim Slimming Treatment – unwanted inches disappear with a herbal gel – were stopped in 1983 *(ASA Case Report 103)*.

HONEY

Honey has long been regarded as a special food. It is the original processed food and yet it is natural – something of a contradiction in terms.

Sugar was little known in most countries, and so expensive that it was restricted to the very rich, until late in the nineteenth century when it became freely available. So for centuries honey was the chief sweetener. Even today we find it remarkable that an insect can collect the nectar from flowers and convert it into honey. How much more mysterious and magical it must have seemed to our forebears. Modern health food claims rely on this ancient mysticism to proclaim the virtues of honey but it is, in fact, little more than a solution of sugars.

Ordinary cane or beet sugar is sucrose. During digestion this is broken down to two simpler sugars: glucose (or grape sugar) and fructose (or fruit sugar). Honey is a 70–75 per cent solution of glucose and fructose; about 2 per cent sucrose, about 0.2 per cent mineral salts, 0.1–0.4 per cent organic acids and the rest, 22–26 per cent, is water with only traces of some vitamins. Its flavour and colour depend on the flowers from which the nectar was obtained.

Despite the fact that honey is only pleasant flavoured sugar many claims are made for it, and entire books have been written on its benefits. It is said to increase human endurance and sexual prowess, as well as having many other virtues, none of which is true.

The 'Organic Food Service' was required by the Advertising Standards Authority to remove its totally untrue advertisement that honey 'retains normal weight and removes fat ... That it speeds up the burning of fat in people in whom this action is slow' *(ASA Case Report 94, February 1983)*.

Not only does honey not possess any unusual nutritional properties, but as with so many other 'natural' foods, it can be toxic. A toxin called grayotoxin has been found in honey which was lethal to rats when injected at a dose level of 1 mg per kg of body weight – about one tenth of a milligram for one rat. Furthermore, if the bees have browsed on certain flowers containing toxins, their honey can be toxic to human beings. In New Zealand, for instance, there were several outbreaks of food poisoning between 1962 and 1967 which were eventually traced to honey made from the Tutu plant (Coriaria arborea) which was heavily infested with the Passion vine hopper (Scolypopa Australia). A toxin produced by the insect passed through the chain until it harmed human beings.

In *A Way of Living as a Means of Survival – An Encyclopaedia of Natural Health*, Michael Wheatley quite incorrectly states that honey is said to be non-fattening as it increases the combustion rate of the body. This is complete nonsense. Honey, being about one quarter water, supplies 3 Calories per gram; pure sugar, having no water, provides 4 Calories to the gram. Nor can honey possibly have any effect on the metabolic rate.

BEES' ROYAL JELLY

If honey has all the properties claimed for it, then how much more magical is bees' royal jelly? This is the substance that changes the larva of the worker bee into a queen bee so it undoubtedly has special properties – at least for the bee. Let us calculate theoretically how much we would need for it to have an effect on human beings. If a bee larva weighs 100 mg and an adult human being weighs 70 kg, then presumably we would have to eat 700,000 times as much as the bee larva does.

The wild claims made for its rejuvenating properties are completely without foundation. It does contain vitamin B6 and another vitamin, pantothenic acid, but since both of these are plentifully supplied in ordinary foods (and can even be bought as tablets from the health food shop), there can be no virtue in buying the jelly. No evidence is offered to support claims that 'extensive medical and scientific research in Europe and America has revealed the remarkable qualities of royal jelly, nature's own rejuvenating food for renewed energy, vitality and youthfulness'. Michael Wheatley *(A Way of Living)* carefully says: 'It is said to help cancer patients.'

In fact, the product was well described several years ago as 'this B nonsense'.

There is a special version – Melbrosia PLD (pour les dames) – and its advertisement quotes a letter from a satisfied customer: 'I started taking Melbrosia PLD about eight years ago ... I am now sixty years of age ... I have for ten years kept a very attractive 6-foot lover by my side!' Perhaps the secret lies in the next testimonial printed immediately below, telling how a housekeeper added two inches to her breasts with the same product. There is also a Melbrosia for men but the difference is not explained – perhaps it is for the King Bee.

INOSITOL

This is a dietary essential for some micro-organisms and so technically can be called a vitamin, although as it is not a dietary essential for humans beings it is not usually classed as such. Chemically it consists of six carbons joined in a ring – once called meat sugar. The garden insecticide, gammexane, works because it is chemically similar to inositol and the insects pick it up, mistaking it for inositol, and die of a vitamin deficiency.

When mice are given diets without any inositol they lose their hair. Rats do not and it has no effect on baldness in human beings. That does not stop health food shops claiming that it cures baldness. And for good measure that it can remove unwanted fat! In fact, although we do not need it in our diet, we get about 1 g a day from our food.

KELP

Kelp is seaweed widely promoted in health food shops, sometimes alone and sometimes in a mixture with vitamin B6, lecithin and/or cider vinegar, coyly called 'the friendly three' (or four).

As with so many health foods the claims made for kelp strain the credulity – it is said to heal every organ in the body.

In an article in the magazine *Here's Health* No. 169, 1972, p. 62 ('your complete monthly guide to health, nutrition, natural foods and natural therapy') the author states that a full list of 'positive results that doctors report would read like a medical encyclopaedia' and 'there are grounds for believing that kelp aids the healing of wounds and broken bones'. In *A Way of Living,* everyone over forty is recommended to take it daily.

The A to Z of Health Food Terms claims that kelp is the 'richest of all foods in mineral content'.

It is even supposed to be good for the garden. The article in *Here's Health* states that vegetables grown in soil manured with seaweed are rich in vitamins and minerals, and of good flavour. In fact, with a few exceptions, plants take whatever minerals they need from the soil and leave the rest behind. They make their own vitamins independently of what is in the soil. In poor soil, plants grow more slowly or are smaller but their nutrient contents stays constant.

There are several hundred varieties of seaweed, but most kelp tablets are made from the bladderwrack (Fucus vesiculosis) or from one of the laminaria. As regards it being rich in nutrients, kelp in fact contains ¾ g of protein and ¾ g fat per 25 g (approximately one ounce) together with 80 mg phosphate, 1.75 g potassium and as much as 1 g – a dangerously high level – of sodium.

Few of the preparations on sale provide any information on the label about the contents. One of the exceptions is Superkelp which contains 3 mg of iodine and 2.5 g of calcium per 25 g. No other ingredients are given. Since one tablet contains only 300 mg of kelp, this would supply 36 micrograms of iodine, not all that much when you consider that we need, and get, about 150–200 micrograms from our daily diet. One tablet would also supply 30 mg of calcium, again not all that much when compared with the 500–600 mg that we need and get from our diet. Even the manufacturers are evidently not satisfied with kelp as a 'rich' source of calcium because they add another 120 mg of calcium to the tablet.

Statements have been made in health food literature, including the article in *Here's Health*, to the effect that kelp contains vitamins A and B (which of the B vitamins is not specified), and vitamins D and E. Even if this were true, the amounts provided by a tablet or so would not be of any significance.

The other components amounting to a 'rich source of minerals' include lead and silver (not so very desirable), traces of manganese (which we get in plenty from a cup of tea), copper (very few people are ever short of copper in their diet), cobalt (of no value to human beings) and magnesium (of which there is no shortage in ordinary foods).

IODINE AND THE THYROID GLAND

Recommendations that people over forty should take kelp daily, and hints that it stimulates the metabolism, are misleading.

Iodine is a dietary essential, needed for the formation of the hormone thyroxine in the thyroid gland, which controls the rate of metabolism of the body. When there is a shortage, either because the diet is deficient or because of substances in the diet that prevent the gland making its hormone, goitre results. This can be seen as a swelling in the neck (an enlargement of the thyroid gland) which is common in people living in certain parts of the world where the soil water is so low in iodine that the plants and animals have too little iodine.

The amount needed daily is about 150 micrograms (one microgram is one millionth of a gram). The majority of the world's population obtains enough iodine from an ordinary diet. Sea fish and all sea foods are particularly rich in iodine. When the hormone thyroxine is insufficient, the metabolic rate is slowed down, but you cannot increase your normal metabolic rate by taking extra iodine. As with most nutrients, enough is enough and there is nothing to gain by taking more. We can increase our metabolic rate with thyroxine but it would be dangerous to do so as the increased metabolic rate would affect the heart.

IS IT SAFE?

To most people the extra iodine, calcium and sodium from kelp tablets would not present any problem (although any extra sodium can be harmful in raising the blood pressure of some people) but there are other, less desirable, substances present as well. In *Martindale's Extra Pharmacopoeia*, reference is made to the presence of arsenic in kelp, as evidenced by the increased excretion of this poison in the urine

80

of people who have taken kelp tablets. Seaweeds are rich in iodine because they concentrate it from sea water, but they also concentrate harmful substances. An article in *CRC Reviews in Food Science and Nutrition (1977, Volume 9, p. 405)* states that kelp contains 100 times as much arsenic as most other foods – 58 parts per million compared with an average value of 0.58 parts per million.

LAETRILE – 'VITAMIN B17'

Laetrile is not a vitamin, although it is sold as such in health food shops. It is an extract of apricot kernels which was claimed as a cancer cure. The stones of apricots, almonds, peaches, cherries and plums (and to a much lesser extent cassava, butter beans, linseed and bamboo shoots) contain chemical substances which are a combination of glucose and cyanide. There are a number of variants called amygdalin and prunasin. Laetrile was originally a derivative of amygdalin which was prepared in the laboratory and patented but never marketed. What was sold as laetrile was in fact an extract of apricot kernels.

When it is heated or treated with strong acid or in the presence of megadoses of vitamin C, the amygdalin breaks down and releases the cyanide. It was widely promoted in the United States as a cure for cancer, with several theories as to why it should work (it does not). One theory was that the cyanide (known in detective novels as prussic acid) goes to the cancer cells and kills them off without affecting the rest of the body. Several deaths and near-deaths from cyanide poisoning from apricot kernels show that it does indeed affect the whole body. Another theory was that cancer was due to a vitamin deficiency which was made good by the amygdalin. That is why it was called, although quite incorrectly, a vitamin.

In fact, the originators did not even have sufficient knowledge of their nutrition literature because vitamins had been numbered up to B15 (which is also not a vitamin), and they jumped straight to B17, missing out 16.

'Vitamin B17' became very popular in the United States and was even smuggled in from Mexico. Since it was dangerous as well as ineffective, a major investigation was carried out in 1978 by the U.S. National Cancer Institute. It had already been banned from interstate commerce by the U.S. Food and Drug Administration as far back as 1971 but public demand forced twenty-seven states to allow its sale. When its use was under violent discussion in the U.S. the purveyors claimed that it had no toxic side effects, but in fact the cyanide content was sufficiently toxic to kill a child, according to a report in the *New England Journal of Medicine (February 1979)*. A healthy eleven month old girl accidentally swallowed between one and five tablets belonging to her father, who believed that because it was a vitamin it was harmless. Within half an hour she became lethargic and began to vomit. When rushed to hospital, her father said the child was suffering from an overdose of a vitamin. Had it been known that it was cyanide poisoning, she might have responded to treatment but by the time the symptoms were recognized, it was too late. The child died from inhibition of respiration due to cyanide poisoning seventy-two hours after taking the tablets.

Two near-deaths were mentioned in a review article in the *Pharmaceutical Journal (17 March 1984, p. 330)*. Two adults consumed twenty apricot kernels purchased from a health food shop and collapsed in a coma for four hours. The article refers to several deaths from this highly promoted 'health product'.

The situation was aptly summarized by a leading article in the *British Medical Journal* as long ago as *1971 (1 January, p. 3)* under the heading 'Laetrile: quacks and freedom'.

Quack cancer cures have been around for a long time. Sooner or later each one is exposed as worthless and is forgotten, but only after a period of notoriety in which the gullible and the desperate may have been cheated out of their money and seen their soaring hopes dashed. So long as conventional medicine cannot cure all patients with cancer, there will be some sufferers willing to try anything that might help.

In America, medicine for the paying patient is in an unhappy state. 'Do you really trust your doctor?' is the name of the game and the number of law suits show the level at which it can be played. In these circumstances it is hardly surprising that laetrile had such a long run in the public eye and was such a source of anger and embarrassment to the Food and Drug Administration, who want to stamp out its use in the United States.

Laetrile production was centred in Tijuana, Mexico where the going rate for an injection was $9, but with an average mark-up of 600 per cent, tablets in the U.S. sold for about $1 each. The Contreras Clinic in Tijuana was estimated to treat some 600 Americans a year at a cost of about $2000 for a course lasting one month. Several American organizations promoted the idea that cancer is a deficiency disease, and they are powerful forces for keeping quack cures in the limelight. Laetrile fulfils their criteria – they can say it is vitamin B17 and the fact that no such vitamin is known to biological science seems to be immaterial.

The attitude of 'health product' vendors and their vendetta against orthodox medicine is illustrated by *When (Alternative Medicine Volume 1, No. 3)* which warned readers against 'propaganda' against laetrile in reports by orthodox medical groups. The writer hopes that 'our readership will be vigilant in spotting and resisting such Establishment propaganda'.

Laetrile never became well known in Great Britain but was sold in health food shops. Because of its dangers, the Department of Health restricted its sales in 1984 (Medicine – Cyanogenetic Substances – Order 1984). The Committee for Safety in Medicines has recommended that it should no longer be allowed to be sold over the counter as a health food supplement.

LECITHIN

Lecithin is another example of a preparation sold in health food shops that is already plentiful in our diet. Our bodies makes as much as we need and any extra simply serves as a source of calories – and rather expensive ones at that. Extra lecithin is of no benefit whatsoever.

WHAT IS IT?
Lecithin is not a single substance, but is the name given to a mixture of fats of a type called phosphoglycerides because they contain phosphate.

Pure lecithins, technically called phosphatidyl cholines (which differ in the types of fatty acids they contain) are never found outside the research laboratory. Commercial lecithin is an impure mixture of the phosphoglycerides that have been extracted from vegetable oils mixed with simple fats (tryglycerides) and some of the oil itself.

WHERE DO WE GET IT FROM?
Commercial lecithin, both that used in many processed foods and the liquid and granules sold in health food shops, is a concentrate made from soya beans. At one time peanuts and eggs were used but they proved too expensive. Some 2–3 per cent of soya bean oil is 'lecithin', about 0.5–1 per cent of sunflower oil and 2 per cent of cottonseed oil. There is quite a lot in our diet already, in eggs, milk, fish, liver and vegetable oils in general. It is used in food processing to help oil and water mix and so is present in chocolate, ice cream, margarine, many cake mixes and baked goods. It is added to 'instant' powders to make them wettable and to frying oils to stop them spattering. So adding tablets to our diet will not add anything worthwhile.

WHAT IS IT FOR?
Lecithins are part of the structure of all cells in the body except for the fatty deposits under the skin – the deposits that make people look fat. They are present in the blood plasma (the clear part) and also in the red blood cells (the blood of an adult contains between 7.5 and 15 g). They are also present in brain and nerve tissues, the kidney, heart and liver.

As they mix with both water and fats they help absorb fat

from foods (lecithin is present in bile which is essential to absorb fat from the intestine into the blood). They also enable fats to be transported around the bloodstream.

WHAT IS CLAIMED?

It is this function of transporting fats around the body that has given rise to some of the unacceptable claims made by health food promoters. They claim that lecithin is a help in slimming because it breaks the fat down into droplets and so helps the body get rid of unwanted fat. This is completely untrue. It is advertised particularly for children, with claims that it provides strength, aids the memory and concentration and improves the appetite.

According to Michael Wheatley (*A Way of Living*) lecithin prevents heart attacks and helps diabetics by reducing the amount of insulin they need. Again, not true. According to Miriam Polunin (*The Right Way to Eat*) lecithin is 'a positive asset to food in the same way as added vitamins would be'. In Ruth Bircher's *Eating Your Way to Health*, it is included with the B vitamins: '. . . yeast extracts . . . are rich in B vitamins e.g. glutathione and lecithin'. Judy Mazel (*The Beverly Hills Diet*) says that pasteurizing milk zaps the lecithin – thus putting a clamp on any hope we might have had of digesting milk; that lecithin is the ingredient that makes eggs digestible; that if lecithin is absent, cholesterol begins to solidify. Lecithin is described (p. 243) as being a key to the digestive enzymes.

Never can so much rubbish have been written about one substance. It is of no value as a food supplement, and as regards slimming claims, lecithin provides 9 Calories to the gram, or 256 to the ounce, so it is fattening if taken in addition to your normal diet.

POLLEN

One of the more mysterious products on sale is pollen – mysterious because its composition is either being kept secret or is not known. Certainly statements made about it differ so much that no nutrient analysis would appear to have been made.

One advertisement says that pollen contains proteins, vitamins, sugar, fat, carbohydrate and enzymes. A report of a 'clinical trial' accompanying the literature of a particular product says that it does not contain any protein, but is rich 'in certain B vitamins'. Another claim is that 'weight for weight pollen contains as much as five times more protein than eggs, cheese or beef'. This is a misleading, not to say illegal, statement. Since beef consists of water, fat and 20 per cent protein, eggs consist of water, fat and 12 per cent protein, and Cheddar cheese is made up of water, fat and 26 per cent protein, it is not difficult to find dried foods, such as milk casein, extracted soya protein, Spirulina (see page 99) and even pollen with more protein 'weight for weight'. The statement is particularly nonsensical when we remember that we eat meat, cheese and eggs by the ounce and pollen, if at all, by the milligram. So any nutrients that it might contain, and no figures are provided, would be of an insignificant amount.

Pollen tablets are claimed to 'have found wide acceptance as having life-giving properties'. This is certainly true of flowers, but why should it be true of human beings?

There is a great deal of competition between manufacturers of the numerous brands of pollen preparations and one particular company makes a special appeal to sportsmen, who are always interested in anything that might improve their performance. The product claims to contain, besides many vitamins, thousands of other substances, including metals which, it is said, can probably be used completely. Furthermore, it says that it is clear that the pollen preparation stimulates hormonal function and contributes to the raising of blood protein. If this were true, not only would it be very dangerous, but it would also, presumably, constitute an illegal use of drugs in athletics. Somewhat alarmingly, the literature adds that Cernitin is practically non-toxic.

There is no doubt that if these pollen preparations became more widely consumed, the manufacturers would have to provide evidence of safety in use. Any novel food of this kind should be tested to show that it is not harmful. Indeed it is harmful since it contains nucleic acids and, as discussed under DNA (page 60), too much of this can cause a rise in blood uric acid levels which is dangerous to health.

PROTEINS AND AMINO ACIDS

WHAT ARE THEY?

Two-thirds of the human body is water, and half of the solid matter is protein, so an average adult has about 10 kg (22 lb) of protein in his or her body. Flesh and blood are largely protein, as are vital organs such as the heart, lungs, liver and kidneys. Indeed, every cell in the human body contains protein, as do all living things whether they are birds, plants, yeasts or bacteria. This means that all food in its original state – such as olives as distinct from olive oil, sugar cane or beet as distinct from sugar, or maize as distinct from custard powder – contains protein and therefore supplies protein for our diet. Obviously the amount of protein differs – 94 per cent in dry, extracted milk casein for instance, 20 per cent in fresh or cooked lean beef, 8 per cent in white bread, 1–2 per cent in boiled potatoes and 1 per cent in leafy vegetables.

All these different proteins, and there are many thousands in the human body as well as thousands more in nature, are made from only twenty basic building bricks, called amino acids. Just as the half million words in the English language are made from various combinations of twenty-six basic letters, so thousands of proteins are made from just twenty amino acids.

The body cannot make amino acids, so they have to be eaten. But how is it that proteins from foods as different as peas, rhubarb and bread can be used to make human tissue proteins? The answer is that proteins are broken down to their constituent amino acids during digestion, and then reassembled by the body to make whatever proteins we need.

Fortunately our bodies are in a continuous state of renewal with about 40 g of protein out of the total of 10 kg broken down each day and replaced by new protein. That is why cuts and wounds heal themselves. That is also why an adult, who has finished growing, needs 40 g of protein in his diet. In fact, we eat on average twice as much as that. Even in the poorest of the developing countries there is no shortage of protein as such. It is food that is in short supply, not just protein. If more food was available, then the requisite quantity of protein would automatically be provided.

Claims made by health food shops trying to sell us proteins and amino acids, then, are frequently untrue, misleading and dishonest.

HOW MUCH PROTEIN DO THEY OFFER US?

The amounts of proteins and amino acids offered for sale must be viewed against the 80 g a day that the average person eats. A product called 1-7-1-Protein powder with FF contains 490 mg of protein. It is claimed: 'This protein supplement enables athletes and body-builders to take advantage of the latest exciting developments in polyunsaturates.' [That is the FF part of the capsule.] 'In combination with lactalbumin [one of the proteins in milk] they [the polyunsaturates] can increase the conversion of proteins still more to give greater muscle potential.' All untrue.

Comfrey is offered for sale as a source of vitamin B12 (see page 73) which 'also contains a high percentage of protein'. But the whole tablet weighs only 500 milligrams altogether.

Vegaprotein contains one single gram of soya protein. It is said to be 'especially useful for vegetarians and vegans where getting sufficient protein is often a problem.' Vegetarians and vegans get plenty of protein from their vegetable sources, so getting sufficient is not a problem, and if it were, an extra gram wouldn't make much difference anyway.

AMINO ACIDS

Of the 40 g of protein that we need a day, about half must supply eight of the amino acids ready-made. They are therefore called the essential amino acids (there are ten essential amino acids for babies, who cannot make the other two). The other twelve can be made in the body from the eight essential ones.

All foods that supply any protein at all contain all twenty

amino acids with the single exception of gelatin (which is extracted from collagen) although the proportions of the amino acids differ. This provides the basis for health food shops to attempt to sell 'essential amino acids', a term which makes them sound very special and very important in the diet.

One product, called Celaton, refers to the amino acids in the product as 'biogenic stimulators', a meaningless term. To make the product sound more valuable it is said to be made from the placenta (afterbirth). As wonderful an organ as the placenta is when it is alive, it is just another mixture of proteins when it has ceased its functioning life. In any case, the tablet contains 1.4 mg of amino acids – about as much as in a crumb of bread. It should be added that Celaton includes some vitamins and mineral salts.

Another product includes the two amino acids methionine and lysine with the claim that they are in short supply in many foods. This is quite untrue. For good measure, the same product includes glutamine, which is a derivative of the non-essential amino acid glutamic acid, plentiful in plant foods. The tablets supply 500 mg.

WHAT IS CLAIMED?

The claims made for these few hundred milligrams of protein and amino acids compared with the 80 g that we eat daily are ludicrous. One of the most striking claims is that: 'There are twenty-two essential amino acids [the wrong number] and if one is missing your hair will not grow.' If one of the essential amino acids was missing from your diet you would be dead and in no position to worry about your hair growing.

On the subject of hair, there are untrue claims for curing baldness and even for making hair grow. There used to be a shampoo on the market which contained hydrolysed porcupine quills, presumably on the basis that if you rub a protein like hair on your head it will make more hair grow. The hydrolysed porcupine quills were prepared by a well-known pharmaceutical firm at great expense, so the makers of the shampoo were not really making any excessive profits.

Another advertisement maintains that: 'most people below par are amino acid deficient', a statement that is both untrue and misleading. The recommended cure is an amino acid mixture and since most customers would not be expected to know that a slice of bread or glass of milk supplies more amino acids than the product – which contains 590 mg of milk casein – they are easily misled. The advertisement boasts that calcium caseinate is 90 per cent protein. So it is, but dried skim milk powder at 36 per cent protein is much cheaper. One slice of white bread contains as much protein as four of these tablets. The story is bolstered by telling potential customers that the product contains eighteen amino acids. Since all proteins contain twenty amino acids, this is hardly useful.

SLIMMING

A wide variety of protein and amino acid preparations are sold as slimming aids for no good reason at all and most of them make illegal claims. Thus Cantaprotein tablets claim to help muscle development and 'do not lead to excessive fat'. This is quite untrue since any food eaten in amounts greater than those used, whether carbohydrate, fat or protein, will lead to fat. If the body cannot burn off the extra calories they must be laid down as fatty tissue. Nor can extra protein in the diet lead to muscular development unless one was short of protein in the first place. Since we already eat at least twice as much protein as we need, any extra cannot do any good.

If you exercise a great deal, your muscles will develop but you do not need to eat extra protein. Even a child, who is not only replacing worn-out protein tissues but also adding to his protein while he grows, needs very little protein each day. If you take a child who gains, say, 3 kg in a year, that is a weight gain of only 8 g per day. Even if it were all muscle protein (and some is fat and bone), that is only about 2 g of protein a day because muscle is three-quarters water. Since the child is eating an average of 20–30 g of protein more than he needs to maintain and repair his tissues, he has this 20–30 g available for the 2 g he needs for growth.

Should you wonder how it is possible that these claims can be described as illegal while the products continue to be sold, the answer is simply that no one has bothered to take action. A complaint to the Trading Standards Officer and also to the Advertising Standards Association would put an end to them.

AMINO ACID IMBALANCE

Each of the twenty amino acids that are found in protein foods can be synthesized in the factory and is on sale in health food shops. These are not only unnecessary but potentially harmful for several reasons.

The addition of too much – as little as a few grams – of any one amino acid to the diet causes an imbalance and results in the loss of protein from the tissues. Methionine, one of the amino acids on sale, has been shown to cause harmful effects in human beings and in experimental animals. The disease pellagra which, as described on page 194, is due to a shortage of the vitamin niacin, can also be caused by adding too much of the amino acid leucine to a poor diet that is low in protein. This is thought to be the main cause of pellagra in parts of India and the Sudan where the principal food is a type of sorghum that is rich in this amino acid.

Finally, too much of some of the amino acids interferes with the penetration of the right mixture into the brain and gives rise to depression. The amino acids sold are in the form of loose powders, which makes dosage difficult. A single teaspoon holds 6 grams and it only takes a very few grams to upset the balance. Yet these chemicals are freely on sale in some 'health' food shops!

RUTIN AND BUCKWHEAT TEA

Orange peel, flowers and many fruits and green leaves contain a group of chemicals collectively called flavonoids. Among the different ones are rutin and hesperidin. They produce the colours in many flowers, fruits and vegetables, so we already have quite a lot in our diet.

When Szent-Gyorgyi, a Hungarian, carried out his early work on vitamin C, he at first thought that an extract of Hungarian peppers, which is very rich in vitamin C, was more effective than vitamin C alone in treating the fragile blood vessels that are the main problem in scurvy. He believed that there was another vitamin present which he called P, both for the 'permeability' of the blood capillaries and for paprika.

Extraction of the peppers in the laboratory showed that they contained several chemically related substances – the flavonoids – which were chemically derived from phenol. Later workers were unable to repeat the result and it is still doubtful whether the flavonoids have any effect at all. They are certainly not essential in the diet, and they are not classed as vitamins, except in health food shops.

The U.S. Food and Drug Administration, with the assistance of the National Research Council, reviewed the use of flavonoids in 1968 and declared that they were not an effective treatment for any condition and recommended their withdrawal.

The recommendation was not put into effect because some doctors thought that there might be a use for them. In the 1967 American Drug Index there were 200 proprietary preparations of rutin or hesperidin. It has been claimed as a cure for the common cold, for nosebleed in racehorses, for food allergies and even for radiation sickness.

In a leaflet on circulation (*No. 9 from Holland and Barrett*) it is claimed that rutin can 'go a long way towards solving four main problems – varicose veins, high blood pressure, hardening of the arteries and capillary fragility'. A leaflet called *Rutin and the Buckwheat Connection* states that: 'extensive experiments both in the U.S.A. and Britain have conclusively demonstrated the efficiency of rutin therapy in the treatment of high blood pressure, vascular disorders and associated problems'. According to *A Way of Living as a Means of Survival*, it is: 'The most famous cure for varicose veins; useful in heart cases to dissolve clots; has been given to animals to prevent cancer deliberately induced by bacteria; prevented miscarriages and bleeding from pernicious anaemia; and used successfully in diseases ranging from colds and rheumatic fever, coronary thrombosis to polio and TB.' This book also states that: 'A symposium held in Russia recently decided that there is no disease state which is not improved by bioflavonoids.' This goes even further than U.S. and UK health food shops.

In Volume II of the textbook *Vitamins in Medicine (1982 edition)* it is stated: 'No condition that can be attributed to bioflavonoid deficiency has ever been demonstrated satisfactorily and it is neither possible nor reasonable to attempt to define a dietary requirement.' This does not prevent it being sold in health food shops together with the rider that it could take four to six months' treatment to have any effect.

In fact, tablets on sale contain 20 or 30 mg of rutin while a single glass of grapefruit juice contains 40 mg and a glass of orange juice twice as much. Tomatoes contain between 85 and 130 mg per 100 g. If you really want a lot, 100 g of onions will provide between 100 and 4000 mg. There is even some in a cup of tea. The average diet supplies 1000 mg daily, so tablets of 20–30 mg can hardly be expected to make any difference. It is also worth knowing that most of it is destroyed by bacteria in the intestine and so very little even gets into the bloodstream.

BUCKWHEAT
The cereal buckwheat (Fagopyrum esculentum) is the food of peasants in central Europe and the middle class in North America, but is not commonly known in Great Britain – the perfect recipe for a 'health food' claim.

Unlike wheat, buckwheat can grow under poor climatic conditions which is why it is common in Russia. The claims made for it are epitomized in *The A to Z of Health Food Terms* where it is described as having 'a particularly high rating for riboflavin'. The standard book *U.S. Composition of Foods* states that the figures for riboflavin in buckwheat are not reliable and none are given. In fact the riboflavin content of all cereals is so low that one could not expect buckwheat to be a rich source. It is also claimed to be rich in iron, whereas in fact it has the same iron content as wheat, 3.1 mg per 100 g.

Buckwheat is described as being a 'very yang grain and one

of the main ingredients of macrobiotic eating'. The reason for including it with rutin is that some rutin preparations are extracted from buckwheat.

SEA SALT

Some very peculiar stories are told about ordinary salt, the pure material, as distinct from sea salt, the impure material. One leaflet distributed through health food shops (*Sunwheel No. 9 published by Sunwheel Foods Ltd.*) states that pure ordinary salt is steam-heated under great pressure to 1200 degrees Fahrenheit and flash-cooled to produce instant crystallization. The resulting salt is not only highly pure, it consists of extremely small crystals that dissolve and ionize poorly and which our bodies find hard to digest. This last part is completely untrue. Water-soluble materials like salt, whether in large and pure or small and less pure crystals, dissolve when taken by mouth. When dissolved, all salts must ionize. To say they are 'poorly ionized' is nonsense and to say that they are 'hard to digest' is even worse because salt is not digested. It is absorbed into the bloodstream exactly as it is, as sodium and chloride.

The same leaflet goes on to criticize table salt because it is made free-running by the addition of magnesium carbonate, and says that iodized salt contains potassium iodide and added glucose to stabilize the iodine and sodium bicarbonate to stop the resulting mixture from turning purple. 'These compounds, like all chemical additives, are potentially harmful to the health.' If that were so then how reprehensible to find the health food shops selling these very same compounds in their separate forms! Magnesium salts are claimed to be valuable to health – in fact, almost everyone obtains more than enough in their food. Iodine is present in the kelp that is so highly prized in the same shops, and dextrose is simply glucose. It so happens that none of these substances is harmful.

Sea salt is also claimed to be a 'balanced food', a term usually reserved for diets supplying all the required nutrients. The term balanced appears from the text to be justified by the presence in sea salt of traces of magnesium, zinc, manganese 'etc.' – these 'valuable minerals' are lost in refining never to be replaced, a claim somewhat at variance with the criticism of the addition of magnesium carbonate to keep table salt free-running.

Such contradictions enable the potential customer to evaluate the dramatic claims made for these various supplements if one takes the trouble to read them carefully.

The real difference between sea salt and ordinary salt is simply dirt. Ordinary white salt is purified sodium chloride, over 99 per cent pure. In some parts of the world it is made by evaporating sea water, in others it is mined. The evaporated sea salt is brown in colour and contains various impurities derived from seaweed, dried shrimps and the general débris of the sea. The penultimate stage is washing these crystals when they become whitish and are 98 per cent pure – the remainder being the dirt from the sea. This is sold as sea salt. Most of it is dissolved and recrystallized to the pure white material that ordinary shops sell.

To stop it caking and blocking the holes in the salt cellar, an 'anti-caking agent' such as calcium or magnesium carbonate or aluminium calcium silicate is added in small amounts. Some salt is sold with added iodide in areas where there is a shortage of iodine in the soil water. That is ordinary salt. Sea salt can cost ten to one hundred times as much.

SELENIUM

Selenium is a mineral that is essential to the diet but which is highly toxic when taken in excess. It was found to be a dietary essential only in 1973 but scientists have known since 1930 that animals grazing on certain pastures developed what was called 'alkali disease' or 'blind staggers' because the grass was so rich in selenium as to be highly toxic.

In man, selenium is part of an enzyme system that protects red blood cells from oxidation. It can, to a certain extent, replace vitamin E in functioning as a fat preservative and so maintain the healthy function of cells. The amount needed is minute – children in certain developing countries who grow poorly were able to achieve a normal rate of growth when as little as 25 micrograms a day was provided. The needs of an adult are thought to be about 33 micrograms a day.

There is plenty of selenium in most foods and it is very rare to find anyone suffering from a deficiency. Nonetheless, extravagant claims are made for selenium tablets – it is claimed to protect against cancer, heart disease, cystic fibrosis and even to promote fertility and long life. Advertisements do admit that we need only minute quantities, but go on to say: 'without it we can succumb to serious illnesses'. Possibly we would, but is anyone going short? Articles in health handouts state, quite incorrectly, that: 'The chances are that you won't be able to get enough just through your diet.' *(Holland and Barrett Express, January/February 1983).* It is strange to think that for so many centuries man lived on food alone, before these magical supplements were invented. The article also states, again incorrectly, that taking supplements is essential. If you are 'one of the people who are rarely ill but who want to get more out of life' the health food stores will sell you a mixture of selenium with vitamins A, C and E. Thus they can attract both customers who are ill, or who think they are, and also customers who are quite well.

SEX AND DIET

When we see articles with titles such as 'Food for Love' and 'The Romance of Food', and particularly when we see that they are written by the authors of romantic novels, we wonder whether it is a leg-pull. From time immemorial man has believed that peanuts, sea-urchin eggs, lettuce, oysters, hedgehogs and pearls dissolved in vinegar will provide the stimulus to sex that so many of us seem to require.

There is serious discussion of the subject in such books as *A*

Way of Living, starting with the definite statement that 'there is no doubt about its [ginseng's] sexual stimulating properties' and 'in this way perhaps it helps to rejuvenate'. The author goes on to say 'the Orientals take it during the winter to keep warm' which might explain the high birth rate in China. The same author incorrectly states that vitamin E is the natural stimulator for sex and 'it works whether you take it in the form of food or as a supplement'. Similarly, he incorrectly maintains that vitamin C taken in large quantities for a period of time (unstated) acts as a stimulant. Also wrong is a statement that excess sweets stimulate sex and that dried fruits and honey (so beloved of health food shops) will have the same effect.

Honey is not always magical when taken by itself, it apparently needs boosting with vitamins. In an article about the magic of honey, the remedy for male impotence and female frigidity is 'breakfast on eggs, bacon and honey followed by two Gev-E tablets, six Healthcraft vitamin E compleat – the life, love and sex vitamin – four Healthcraft vitamin A compleat – which is essential for male potency and affects the semen – three Celaton CH3 plus – the virility tablet, and two dessertspoonsful of Quintessence.' One might wonder how children were ever born before health food supplements were invented.

It may be relevant to point out that in macrobiotics 'frequent change of sexual and physical vitalities are [thank goodness] both yin and yang combined'. Excessive sexual libido is yang, so one must therefore eat more yin foods to overcome this so-called disorder of the reproductive system! The rapid increase in the population of the world in the twentieth century is attributed to the wider use of yang foods, notably refined grains, sugar, 'semi-treated food', semi-tropical and tropical fruits, dairy foods, potatoes, tomatoes and chemically treated foods. It is recommended that a return to regional products would stabilize the population. This apparently means that we should eat whatever grew in our locality before other kinds of food were introduced.

International Planned Parenthood Association please note.

Among the way-out ideas that always get radio and television coverage was that of a French gynaecologist in February 1984. It sounds more like a hoax than anything else, but a Dr Papa(!) claimed that a diet rich in potassium and sodium makes little boys and a diet rich in calcium and magnesium makes little girls if those foods are eaten by the intending mother before conception. Since there is always a one-in-two chance of having a boy or a girl, any theory linking diet and the sex of babies could be right.

WOMEN'S LIB

What is sauce for the goose does not appear to be sauce for the gander in health food shops. They sell special preparations for men which differ, although we are not always told how, from those sold for women.

You can buy that magical stuff called bees' royal jelly specially formulated for men (see page 77). Even that ancient remedy of all life's ills, ginseng, is not equally suitable for the two sexes. Larkhall Laboratories advertise a special replacement of ginseng for women. 'In the Orient ginseng is taken by men but women have used Dong Quai root for the same purpose for thousands of years ... So for the ladies who have been mistakenly using men's ginseng, now you have your own special herb from the East.' The Vitasafe Plan sells tablets with twenty-five 'laboratory tested' ingredients but twenty-six under the women's plan.

There are one or two health food supplements that are labelled 'for adults only'. Since the label does not indicate any reason why children should not take them, this warning is presumably intended as a selling gimmick.

Readers particularly interested in sex and sexual stimulants may already have patronized one or more sex shops. Look at the labels of the special and expensive preparations that do 'so much good' and you will see that they are just vitamin pills, cheaper to purchase in food or even health food shops, and just as ineffective.

SPIRULINA

Spirulina is a minute plant, an alga, that floats on lakes and ponds. It was not discovered by Western scientists until 1962 but it has been eaten for centuries by North Africans living around Lake Chad and by Mexicans since the time of the Aztecs.

Spirulina has the most useful facility of growing almost by itself. As a plant it gets its energy from sunshine and its carbon dioxide from the air. It gets its mineral salts from the water in which it grows, but one of its outstanding features is that it makes its nitrates from the nitrogen in the air. So it does not need anything supplied to it by the farmer.

Such a potential food source for the developing countries naturally aroused considerable interest in the Food and Agriculture Organization of the United Nations and a great deal of research has been carried out over the past twenty years.

What a good story for the health food movement! They can even say that it made its début on earth three million years ago. But the facts themselves were not good enough, they had to be embroidered. Claims are now made that spirulina is the world's richest source of protein. Calculated on dry matter it contains 62–68 per cent protein, but compare this with 97 per cent for white fish, 90–96 per cent for various preparations of milk casein, 80 per cent for chicken and 79 per cent for lean beef.

It is also claimed that 'among natural foods researchers have never found anything that has a higher vitamin content' (this as well as its abnormal protein content!) but spirulina contains no more carotene than other green vegetables, and much less than carrots. The B vitamins are at about the same levels as those in dried yeast and there is only a trace of vitamin C. The only statement that is true is that it is one of the rare plant sources of vitamin B12, and as such it is useful for vegans.

Spirulina is proclaimed as a slimming aid because it is rich in one amino acid, phenylalanine, an appetite depressant. In fact it is no richer in this amino acid than most other proteins and there is no evidence that it depresses the appetite.

The term 'only' was cleverly used by *Healthy Life News of Australia (January 1984)* when saying that spirulina only contains 3.9 Calories per gram. Clearly they do not expect customers to know that sugar contains only 4 Calories to the gram and that bread contains only 2 Calories to the gram.

Some of the claims don't even make sense; for example: 'If one takes spirulina regularly its high protein and nourishments can change one's acidic body fluid into basic, help rebalance one's deviated nutrious condition, strengthen healing and defensive powers against sickness and bring back a strong and healthy physical condition.'

As the product caught on among the gullible, more and more manufacturers appeared and their claims became even wilder. A dose of 1–2 g cured everything from wrinkles and shortness of breath when climbing stairs to hives, asthma and white hair in young people (not, apparently, in old people). It was also claimed to be an aphrodisiac. One advertisement stated: 'If you don't find an improvement then your physical quality was basic and healthy already. You should be happy with that.' This was apparently aimed at dissatisfied customers.

Spirulina was supposed to be rapidly absorbed into the bloodstream, although in fact it is relatively poorly digested because of the cellulose cell walls. It was this rapid absorption, apart from the presence of the amino acid phenylalanine, that was alleged to help slimmers by controlling their blood sugar – all this with a gram or less of a vegetable! Curiously enough one brand even claims to be produced artificially.

Almost every health food manufacturer, large and small, and certainly all health food shops, got in on the racket and it had to be stopped. Action has now been taken by the authorities in various countries.

In the *Newsletter of the California Council Against Health Fraud (May/June 1982)* it was reported that the founder of the microalgae company had made an out-of-court settlement of $225,000 for claiming that spirulina has therapeutic effects on diabetes, anaemia, liver disease and ulcers. 'One person weighing 128 lb could live for 17 years off one drum of spirulina and one person of 180 lb needing 22.5 g of protein a day (this is half the actual amount needed) could live for 12½ years.'

An advertisement for spirulina in Great Britain stated that a spirulina/hypothalamus diet discovery allows weight loss of 7 lb and more. The objection to this claim was upheld by the Advertising Standards Authority (*ASA Case Report 99, July 1983*). Another advertisement for slimming was accompanied by the letters Med. Sc. Reg. and I.A.S. after the name of the advertiser. The Advertising Standards Authority (*ASA Case Report 99, July 1983*) questioned the meaning of these letters and it turned out that I.A.S. was a misprint for I.H.S. which stands for International Health Society, and Med. Sc. Reg. referred to a certificate the advertiser had from Medscan of Leeds. Since neither of these sets of letters represents generally recognized qualifications, the Authority decided that this could be misleading and the advertiser agreed not to use them in future.

We have certainly not seen the last of spirulina. Advertisers will change the wording each time they are challenged, and with the list of claims they have already made in leaflets, books, magazines and advertisements, their brainwashed customers will continue buying it. Its only virtue, a plant source of vitamin B12, is being swamped by the mountain of magic.

SUGAR – NATURAL OR NOT?

No one, apart from sugar public relations companies, and health food stores, suggests that 'sugar is good for you'. It tastes pleasant and plays an important part in the composition and texture of a great many foods, but it is not essential in the diet nor does it have any special nutritional virtues. But health food suppliers would have us believe that 'natural sugar', that is sugar in dried fruits, is good for us. They even advertise fruit bars 'free from added sugar'. Indeed, they are free from added sugar, but that is because they do not need additions, they are already full of sugars.

Grapes contain 15 per cent sugars and by the time they have been dried to make raisins and currants they contain 64 per cent sugar – about the same amount as in jams and syrups. Dried dates, hallowed by biblical quotations and eaten by primitive peoples, contain 64 per cent sugars, while dried figs contain 53 per cent. Honey (see page 75) is simply sugar and water – three quarters sugar and one quarter water.

There is (or was) a dried fruit bar on sale in Great Britain called NutriDelite manufactured in the United States and imported from West Germany (and the health food magazines denigrate multinational companies!). It is labelled 100 per cent natural fruit bar with 'no sugar added'. The 50 g bar supplies 187 Calories, nearly one tenth of the average daily consumption of food. This works out at 3.74 Calories per gram – exactly the same as pure, crystalline glucose and more than golden syrup at 3.0 Calories per gram and jam at 2.6 Calories. The label also states 'in low-calorie rice-wafer' which is true but misleading.

What seems to be a similar product was the cause of a complaint laid against an advertisement by Brewhurst Food Supplies (*ASA Case Report 102, October 1983*). The product was advertised in *Here's Health*, a leading magazine in the health food industry, under the heading 'You won't spoil yourself' and stated 'most people who are concerned with their health tend to shy away from sweets. Yet the temptation to bite into something chewy can sometimes be unbearable. With Bellis fruit bars you can chew to your heart's content without thinking twice about your health. Nutritious Bellis bars are made from natural unprocessed Australian dried fruits, nuts and honey.' The complainant, a medical herbalist, had found that the product included added glucose and sugar. The defence was that the advertisement did not make any specific claims that the product was sugar-free and pointed out that the wrapper on the fruit bars clearly listed the ingredients. The Authority did not accept the defence.

They were not concerned, of course, with the fact that so large a concentration of sugars in the dried fruits was no less (or more) harmful than any preparation containing the same amount of added sugar, nor that fruits lose all or most of their vitamin C and vitamin A (carotene) on drying so that the apparent nutritional attractions of fruit are reduced mostly to sugar and dietary fibre.

SUCROSE, GLUCOSE AND FRUCTOSE
Ordinary table sugar, whether it comes from the sugar cane or the sugar beet, is sucrose. By the time it has been digested and enters the bloodstream, it has been separated into its two constituents, glucose and fructose. Fruits contain glucose (also called grape sugar) and fructose (called fruit sugar), as does honey. Even lemonade drinks, sweetened with sugar when manufactured, very soon change to glucose and fructose in the bottle through the acids present. So it doesn't matter whether you eat purified cane or beet sugar, or the purified and extracted glucose and fructose, or the dried fruits so rich in glucose and fructose – so far as our nutrition is concerned, they are all the same.

BROWN OR WHITE?
It does not matter whether the sugar on the table is brown or white. Both are very nearly pure sucrose and the brown contains only very small traces of mineral salts (and smaller traces of B vitamins) too small to do any good. The very dark sugar, the least pure, is 91–96 per cent sucrose (with 2–4 per cent water) compared with the very white sugar which is 99.9 per cent sucrose.

The only types of sugar which do supply appreciable amounts of nutrients are the first stages of the final purification from the raw material, that is the black-strap molasses and black treacle which do not crystallize. Black treacle can supply as much as 20 mg of iron in 100 g (compared with a recommended daily intake of 10–15 mg) and about 350 mg of calcium (compared with a recommended daily intake of

600 mg). By the time it has been purified up to the stage of dark brown sugar the levels are reduced to one tenth of this amount and by the time the lighter brown sugars are reached, the amount of minerals is too small to be of any nutritional significance.

The B vitamins are present only in small amounts, even in the cruder extracts. The general belief that brown sugar is 'better' than white reflects the fact that brown bread contains more nutrients than white bread. This is not true of sugars.

Health food shops are very confused about sugar. Some leaflets condemn all sugar, some condemn the white but think the browns are nutritious. They all seem to believe that sugars 'naturally' present in dried fruits are good. The confusion is exemplified by claims made about natural versus sweetened yoghurt. What is called natural yoghurt in Western Europe is unsweetened and relatively acid to taste. It is not very popular and most people buy the sweetened, fruit-flavoured varieties. In *When – Alternative Medicine (Volume 1, No. 3)*, one writer admits that people may not like the acidic flavour of the 'better' natural varieties and suggests that this taste can be overcome by adding honey or brown sugar. So you finish up exactly where you would have been had you bought the already sweetened yoghurt.

The confusion in health food leaflets is further compounded by a quite inexplicable claim made for Gaylord Hauser's black-strap molasses. This is said to contain seven times more natural iron than calories. The meaning of this claim cannot even be guessed at.

HALVA
Halva is a sweet made from sesame seed, glucose and honey, originating in the Mediterranean countries. Health food promoters advertise a new version as being sugar-free because it is made from sesame seeds and honey. Since honey is three quarters fructose and glucose, the halva is neither nutritionally better than the older variety, nor is it sugar-free.

'VITAMIN B15'

Laboratory experiments are not always easy to interpret. Sometimes results cannot be confirmed because the conditions are not exactly the same or there can be several different explanations to one set of results. Where living material is used, whether animals, bacteria, plants or pieces of tissue in a test tube, there are so many unknown influences that the scientist sometimes gets a result that he himself cannot explain. These are some of the reasons why any single scientific claim is looked at with scepticism until other workers have been able to confirm the findings.

This is one possible explanation of why people sometimes think they have discovered a new vitamin – something that is essential to a living organism – but later find that they were mistaken. For example, there is no vitamin B3, B4 or B5 because those names were assigned by the original experimenters to substances that later turned out to be known chemicals or a mixture of chemicals which were later separated.

So it was with vitamin B15. The original laboratory worker had a substance that he found, in the test tube, to be involved in the oxidation processes that proceed in living cells. He called it vitamin B15 but since it is not a dietary essential it is not a vitamin. It is a real substance however and is called pangamic acid.

Health food salesmen could not resist the chance to sell this 'new vitamin'. They promote it as the 'feel good' pill and claim that it can cure fatigue, alcoholism, schizophrenia, heart disease and allergies and (of course) reverse the aging process.

There is a grain – and a very small one it is – of truth beneath this tissue of fabrication. Pangamic acid is concerned with oxidation processes. The copywriters have jumped to the conclusion, quite without justification, that it must therefore increase the amount of oxygen in the blood and so do good.

According to reports in the *Journal of the American Medical Association (1980, Volume 243)* and the *American Journal of*

Clinical Nutrition (1979, Volume 32), what is often sold in the United States under the label of vitamin B15 is not even pangamic acid, but whatever the salesman puts in the bottle. In the United States it is now illegal to sell substances called vitamin B15 but there are no such inhibitions in Great Britain and Australia where there is always someone, usually a public figure in the world of sport or entertainment, who will provide a testimonial. They may even genuinely feel that whatever they have taken did them good – see the placebo effect (page 8).

FACTS AND CLAIMS

Consumers are regularly advised by government agencies, nutrition educators and food scientists to read the labels on packets of food. Few of us do so. If we did, we might well ask why packets of kelp sold in the health food shop do not state how much iodine they contain, or what it is in the mixture of vitamins that can possibly cause weight loss, or what are the ingredients of preparations such as pollen and bees' royal jelly.

As explained elsewhere, products (including vitamins) sold in health food shops are not controlled in the same way as those products (including vitamins) sold in pharmacies under the Medicines Act but merely have to conform to the labelling regulations.

The regulations controlling foods do not allow misleading or exaggerated claims and the local authority, through the Trading Standards Officer, can call for evidence of such claims. The Advertising Standards Authority will ban advertisements that make claims that are inaccurate, misleading or cannot be substantiated. Health food products, however, get round all these regulations by writing articles in free newspapers and 'health' magazines which are not classed as advertisements and are presumably the opinion of the author. The author is usually a health food supporter and it is more than interesting to note that many of the magazines are owned by the same organizations which make and sell the health foods.

So it is possible to read all about non-existent vitamins such as B15 and B17 and the unsubstantiated claims for the virtues of supplements and extracts.

VITAMINS FOR EVERYTHING

There are three areas of human hope that ensure good sales – sex, slimming and health. While vitamins, as described in Chapter 6, do have remarkable properties, it is stretching the truth to claim that they can fulfil all three hopes, particularly with the same mixtures.

Sex shops sell tablets that will provide the expected vim and vigour but if we take the trouble to read the labels, it becomes apparent that the packs contain nothing but simple vitamin tablets.

Slimming is discussed in Chapter 7, but it is worth mentioning here that several so-called 'slimming preparations', all of which are illegal in Great Britain with unacceptable claims, are just vitamin tablets.

Finally, there are claims made for healthy minds and bodies which again refer to simple vitamin mixtures. We could probably get as much benefit, if not even more, from a good meal as we could from some of these preparations. Take, as an example, Ayurvedic Health Tonic which keeps your body healthy for longer by slowing down wear of tissues; improves mental development; has anabolic properties; builds up immunity and is useful in the treatment of colds, coughs, asthma and tuberculosis. It is based on Indian mythology according to which the physicians of the gods prescribed it to restore the great Rishi Chyavana to youth when his vitality was ebbing. According to the label, the tonic consists of vitamin C and niacin; tests 'show a positive reaction for vitamins A and E' (this probably means that small traces are present); a full adult dose contains 135 mg of protein (compared with the average daily intake of about 80 g), 6 g carbohydrate and a variety of mineral salts, namely calcium, iron, manganese, phosphorus, copper and zinc. All this is provided in a natural form from the amla fruit – full name Amblemyrobelon – presumably Emblica officinalis or Indian gooseberry. In an attempt to provide a scientific basis for the product the label states that it is only for the use of registered medical practitioners and hospital doctors – yet it is also on sale to the public!

FREE PUBLICITY

Much of the blame for spreading food myths, scares and old wives' tales undoubtedly lies with the media. The moment a crank signals a sensational announcement, he is given all the publicity the Press, radio and television can muster. Sensation is news. Fact, unless it is stranger than fiction, is not.

It is human nature to remember the sensational and forget later evidence to the contrary, retractions or apologies. In Chapter 1 I mentioned the gullible Americans who wanted access to a cancer cure even after it had been proved useless. Television producers and newspaper editors know full well what the public wants to hear.

In 1975 I participated in a violent argument on Thames Television with someone who claimed that his 'patient' lived without food or water, purely on cosmic nourishment. This was generated to him through constant telephonic communication with a lady in Berchtesgaden, Germany (a place many readers will remember). The press handout stated that cosmic nourishment is a system of nourishing the body without food or drink for periods of time much greater than those generally accepted by the medical profession. Indeed, this claim was the main cause of the violence of the argument conducted during the programme. The claimant stated that his subject had gone without food, water or any fluid for six weeks – totally impossible. The press release rightly stated that this cosmic nourishment is 'clearly relevant to the world's hunger problem'. As so often happens with claims for health cures this was supported by 'doctors from a Swiss clinic'. The press release said that two people had lived for eleven days and one for seven days without food or drink but during the programme it was claimed that another person lived for six weeks and was healthier than when he started.

A slightly less dramatic argument was conducted on BBC radio. A medical scientist visiting this country stated that everyone is suffering from a shortage of vitamins, but samples of hair, skin and tissues could be analysed so that each individual's vitamin needs could be identified. There is an obvious fallacy to his suggestion, however. What deficiency could be diagnosed if, between the day of testing and the following day you were to eat half a pound of carrots (one month's supply of vitamin A), a serving of liver pâté (one week's supply of several B vitamins) or a glass of fruit juice (several days' supply of vitamin C)?

The irresponsibility of the media in giving publicity to such claims was emphasized by the programme itself. First, it was stated that a great discovery had been made, namely that everyone is short of vitamins. Second, this information, along with details of how it could be diagnosed and rectified, was said to be published in a book available to the public although no scientific evidence had ever been published in a single professional journal. Finally, the claimant admitted that he had not yet produced any scientific evidence but said that after eight years he was *then* going to investigate the truth of his claims and 'as a good scientist' (his words) would then retract if found wrong.

EVIDENCE

Very few manufacturers of health supplements, organically grown foods and various cures offer evidence of their usefulness. Statements about their value do not constitute evidence. Nor do claims that 'everyone knows'. Once upon a time 'everyone knew' that the world was flat and even medical men 'knew' that drawing blood helped a patient recover from fever.

Unfortunately for the truth, many of us believe what we want to believe and are more than ready to accept claims that this or that product will confer long life, sexual prowess or abundant health even when the claims are as farfetched as some quoted here.

WHY DON'T YOU COMPLAIN?

There are numerous regulations which exist to protect the consumer, but the consumer does not always know about them. Complaints about any goods may be taken to a local Trading Standards Department or in some instances the Environmental Protection Department. The Advertising Standards Authority advertises its own activities regularly.

In the area of health foods, several products have been reported and appropriate action subsequently taken. One problem is that claims are sometimes made in articles and editorial matter – which is not illegal.

An advertisement that Biotherm would help towards a firmer outline around areas prone to cellulite, especially the hips, knees and thighs, was defended by the statement that this was a promotion by the magazine, organized and written by the publishers. The publishers stated that there had been a misunderstanding. The reader's complaint was upheld (*ASA Report 89, September 1982*).

The London Natural Health Clinic was criticized because it claimed to treat 'hay fever, sinusitis, fibrosis, skin complaints, dietary problems, arthritis, sexual problems, restricted movement, migraine, cigarette addiction, stiff neck, tennis elbow, high blood pressure, backache, stomach upsets, sports injuries, tiredness' – the modern equivalent of the nineteenth-century American snake doctor!

The Clinic was informed by the Authority that references to skin diseases, arthritis, sexual problems, migraine, high blood pressure and backache were proscribed by the Code of Practice in Advertising.

Some of these claims are so wide-ranging that it does not seem possible to substantiate them. Vebo (UK) Ltd. advertised a health product that is good for the brain, steadies the nerves, stimulates the liver, strengthens and keeps the heart young, helps the stomach, retards aging, helps disorders of sleep and is also good for overstrain ... using well-tried and clinically proven active ingredients. Such spurious scientific wording does appear rather convincing but the advertisement had to be withdrawn (*ASA Case Report 94, February 1983*).

Apart from employing scientific terms which could easily persuade the layman, the purveyors of health foods appear to read the scientific literature in order to pick up anything potentially usable, whether it be a suggestion by an individual, a preliminary finding, a hypothesis or a verified scientific fact. Any tentative research finding may be seized upon as a proven scientific fact to promote sales. One such is 'chelation' – an approach which, according to *Healthy Life News of January 1984*, was at that time sweeping Australia. Gardeners may know about chelation – plants that dislike lime in the soil can grow in such soil if a chemical chelating agent is added to bind the calcium. Many mineral salts can be chelated and in some instances, such as that of iron, this leads to a greater degree of absorption of the mineral from food into the bloodstream. According to *Healthy Life News* in a review of a book on the subject, there is a 'frightening conspiracy undertaken against chelation in the medical world' apparently because the medical world would otherwise be deprived of the profits of coronary by-pass operations!

There are on sale what are called vitamin-mineral bridges. These are complexes between a chemical called orotic acid (and claimed in health articles to be a vitamin) and mineral salts such as iron orotate and magnesium orotate.

Such artificial compounds, surely the antithesis of the natural approach advocated by the health food business, sound scientifically attractive. There is no evidence that such orotate compounds are any better absorbed than any other form of mineral salt eaten in food. We do know that iron is better absorbed in the presence of proteins, fructose and certain other foodstuffs because it is chelated with those foods but we have no evidence that these orotates are not broken down during digestion and so lose any chelating benefit.

4

VALUE FOR MONEY

PACKAGING

People buy food and diet supplements in health food shops because of the claims made for them. The food is usually advertised as being superior to 'ordinary' food which is condemned because it is 'mass-produced, over-processed and over-packaged'. Many people are apparently willing to pay more for the products of health food shops to attain these so-called superior qualities.

It is not at all clear what over-packaging means. Packaging is intended to protect food from contamination, physical damage, loss of nutritive value through exposure to air and moisture, as well as to provide a label to carry the information required by both the law and the consumer. Certainly all manufacturers – including those of health foods – like to make their packets and cans stand out so they often indulge in packaging that is supposed to be attractive. The worst that can be said about such packaging is that it increases the price to the consumer, but this increase is usually negligible. There are in fact very few examples of over-packaging on supermarket shelves. While that charge can justifiably be levelled at non-food products, such as men's shirts and cosmetics in which the packaging is often excessive and does indeed comprise a significant part of the final cost, it is not often true of food containers. Even a gaudy label costs very little more than a plain one so there is little, if any, extra cost to the consumer.

PROCESSING

Food evangelists use such terms as processed and over-processed indiscriminately, with little or no understanding of their meaning. Almost every food we eat is processed to some extent. Indeed, cooking itself is a process.

There are very few foods that are not subjected to some degree of treatment. At the bottom end of the scale is the process of cooling or chilling, defined as temperatures between 5 and -1 degree C. Meat was one of the first foods to be transported around the world in a chilled form, but it is also widely used for dairy produce, eggs, fish, fruit and vegetables to extend their life by anything from a few days (milk) to several weeks (meat, bacon, cheese). Chilling was used by the ancient Romans who collected ice during the winter in order to keep their food cool in caves during warmer weather. The death of Francis Bacon some 1500 years later was attributed to exposure to cold when he got out of his coach in bad weather to test the effect of chilling a chicken by filling it with snow. When does cooling in such an 'artificial' way by man become a process any different from the 'natural' effect of cold weather? Somewhat further along the line is the storage of fruit and vegetables in a controlled atmosphere known as 'controlled-gas-storage'. Officially designated CA for controlled atmosphere storage, or MA for modified atmosphere storage, it is achieved by reducing the proportion of oxygen by increasing the carbon dioxide. It is applied to fruit and vegetables during storage and transport. Although technically clever, it is not a very extreme method of food processing.

Next on the scale of 'interference' by man with natural fresh foods is freezing. For this process food must first be blanched, i.e. immersed in boiling water, or otherwise heated for a few minutes to destroy the enzymes that would continue to function even at low temperatures. The food is then cooled to somewhere between -18 and -30 degrees C where it can be kept for months and even years.

Since food deterioration is caused both by the breakdown of tissues by natural enzymes as well as by attack from bacteria, moulds and yeast, another method of preservation is to heat the food sufficiently to destroy the enzymes and harmful bacteria but not so severely as to destroy all the bacteria. This is pasteurization as opposed to sterilization. Pasteurized food will keep for only a few weeks. Complete sterilization is more severe and must be accompanied by protection of the food from later contamination from bacteria, yeasts or mould by enclosing it in a tin or bottle. So canning and bottling are relatively severe methods of processing.

Another process widely used is the milling of grain. Few people enjoy eating wheat grains so they are processed by being ground into flour. And since not many people enjoy eating flour, this in its turn is processed, with the addition of such unusual materials as yeast and salt, to make bread.

The only possible explanation of the term 'over-processed' would seem to apply to white flour. The grinding of wheat grains into flour is a process and its further conversion into white flour could be regarded as over-processing. Fewer people in Great Britain eat wholemeal bread than white – about one family in twenty eats wholemeal – so wheat is processed even further by removing the germ and the outer layers of bran to produce white flour and consequently white bread. This more highly processed white bread is nutritionally inferior to the less highly processed wholemeal loaf, with brown bread coming in between – but all bread is a processed, indeed a convenience, food.

There are also some less common processed foods such as expanded or spun soya beans. In the case of expanded soya, the bean is crushed and its fat extracted. The defatted soya flour is then made into a batter with water, and colours and flavours are added before the batter is passed through a pressure chamber where it is heated to a temperature above the boiling point of water. Since it is under pressure the water cannot boil; when the pressure is released, the water suddenly turns to steam and blows bubbles in the batter.

A much more sophisticated process is used to spin soya. Here the soya flour is dissolved in very strong caustic soda and squirted through very fine holes into a solution of acid to neutralize it. When this happens, the solution of soya protein is precipitated and since it comes out of the holes in a long thin jet, the precipitated protein is in fine hairlike strands. Several thousand of these fine holes are bored in a block of metal so that when the hair-like strands of protein are produced they are packed close together and actually look like a lock of blonde hair. Colours and flavours can be added to the solution of protein before it is 'spun' or added to the product afterwards to make it look and taste something like meat.

This, indeed, is a very highly processed food. It is sold in Britain primarily in health food shops, where leaflets and magazines are distributed denigrating highly processed foods.

PROCESSING
AND NUTRITIONAL VALUE

Some nutrients are always lost when food is processed – or cooked. If you were to ask me whether processed foods are 'as good as those Mother used to make', I would have to answer 'it depends on your Mother'!

Some mothers are very good cooks and prepare food which is superior in every way to that produced in factories, or even in the best restaurants. Others are not so good. But any well-organized food factory under the direction of a good food technologist should be able to produce food of an equal if not better quality, in terms of nutrition and flavour, than that turned out by many home cooks.

The nutrient that is most easily damaged in processing is vitamin C. It is equally susceptible to damage during cooking. The B vitamins are also water-soluble, which means that part is washed out into the processing or cooking water. The amount lost depends on how finely the food is chopped.

Vitamin C is damaged by heat in the presence of air, particularly if any copper or iron vessels are used, so there can be large losses in fruit or vegetables that have been frozen, canned or dried. But the bigger problem is that fruit and vegetables containing vitamin C also contain the enzyme that destroys it. In the living plant this enzyme is separated from the vitamin, but as soon as the plant leaves or fruit are harvested, the cell walls begin to break down and the enzyme comes into contact with the vitamin and begins to destroy it.

Some leafy vegetables can lose vitamin C very quickly in warm conditions. Kale, for example, can lose 1½ per cent of its vitamin C every hour – which is one third lost within a day of harvesting. A series of measurements in Nigeria showed that leafy vegetables picked at 8 a.m. had lost 90 per cent of their vitamin C by early afternoon.

When vegetables are bruised or wilt after they have been harvested, or when food is cut up so that the enzyme can make contact with the vitamin, the damage begins. Finely chopped cabbage, sliced tomatoes and most fresh fruit and vegetables can lose a large part of their vitamin C in the hour or so before they are eaten.

The enzyme, like all other enzymes, is destroyed by heat, so when food is cooked – or canned, or blanched before freezing or drying – the destruction of vitamin C is halted. That is why home economists tell us to drop cabbage into boiling water, and not to put it into cold water and then bring it up to the boil.

Potatoes slowly lose vitamin C during storage after the autumn harvest in Western Europe. They start out in October with about 30 mg per 100 g – which is quite a lot when you consider that we eat from 250 to 500 g in one meal. Although they lose their vitamin C at a slower rate than leafy vegetables, by early spring nearly one third has gone. This is one of the reasons why scurvy was common in England and Europe in early spring centuries ago. The other reason was that there were few fruits and vegetables available before the possibility of importing them from other countries during the winter became practical, and before canning, drying under controlled conditions and freezing became commonplace.

After all the losses which take place when vegetables are stored, cut and cooked, there can be an even greater loss of vitamin C if food is kept hot after it is cooked. When potatoes are boiled they lose only a little of their vitamin C. The greatest loss occurs when you are late for a meal and the mashed potatoes have to be kept hot – they lose about half of their vitamin C every twenty minutes. So if you are an hour late, you will be left with a half of a half of a half – that is just one eighth – of what was left after storage and cooking.

So much for the fresh, unprocessed potato as a source of vitamin C. The vitamin B1 in potatoes is much more stable, and the protein, mineral salts and starch are unaffected by all this. It is only the vitamin C that is severely damaged.

It is easy to see, then, why when fruit and vegetables are frozen, canned, bottled or dried under factory conditions it is often possible to find that the finished product actually contains more vitamin C than the so-called 'fresh' food cooked at home. The manufacturer of processed foods can almost always obtain his fresh foods fresher than the housewife can. The fruit and vegetables we buy from a retail shop often come from a wholesaler who obtained them from a nearby farm. They will at best be a day or two old, and at worst several weeks old. The manufacturer can process food within a few hours of harvesting it. He is able to start with food containing more vitamin C than the housewife's purchases and, what is more, his food technologists should know more than most housewives about how to process the food without too great a loss of vitamin C. Processing does result in an initial loss, but after that the vitamin C keeps well in canned, frozen or dried food. So in some instances processing can be an advantage nutritionally, apart from making food available in quantity all year round.

Now how do health food claims about processed and 'over-processed' foods sound?

ORGANIC FARMING

Claims that organically produced foods are nutritionally better than those conventionally grown were discussed in Chapter 2. However, most discussions of the differences between the two methods conclude 'if you prefer the taste of

118

organically grown food despite the extra cost then that is your personal decision'. But are the claims that organically grown food tastes better than the 'mass produced' ordinary foods true?

Scientists can analyse food for its texture, freedom from bacteria and nutritional content, but, apart from analysing it chemically for flavouring substances, they must leave decisions about taste preferences to the consumer. Tasting experiments conducted from time to time on organically-manured food, free-range chickens or their eggs and food grown without the use of agricultural chemicals demonstrate that they are not preferred to ordinary food. In most cases, they could not be distinguished from 'mass produced' food. Indeed in some tests the ordinary food was selected in preference to the 'special' varieties.

HOW TO TASTE

It is vitally important that tasting trials are carried out under fully controlled conditions in which the participants cannot be influenced by price and appearance. There have been trials in which jam was put into tall, narrow jars, making it look paler than it did in short, fat jars. The tasters unanimously preferred the jam in the short fat jars 'because it contained more fruit'.

Similar trials have compared milk chocolate with plain. The preference was for the chocolate labelled milk – when the labels were switched, so were the preferences.

Even experts can be misled by colour and appearance. Food scientists experienced in tasting cannot detect flavours when the 'wrong' colour is used. On two occasions several years apart members of the Food Group of the Society of Chemical Industry were entertained by being offered sweets coloured red when lemon flavoured, yellow when raspberry flavoured and green when strawberry flavoured. They were unable to identify the flavours correctly. In a similar test, ice cream was offered – the coffee flavour was white, chocolate was pink and the vanilla brownish. Again, the tasters could not identify the flavours.

Slightly browned, dried 'green' vegetables have been rejected by expert taste panellists but accepted when they were offered again under coloured lights.

Which is why it is essential to conduct tests under conditions in which the taster, and the people carrying out the tests, are unaware of the source, name and price. Such a test was carried out by three home economists and dietitians at the Good Housekeeping Institute and published in *Nutrition (1962)*. Participants were asked to tell the difference and express a preference from among the following:

1 oranges grown on organically fertilized soil compared with mineral salts;
2 free-range compared with battery chickens;
3 raspberry and blackcurrant jams, made with fruit that was organically fertilized or with mineral salts.

Each food was assigned a letter so that it could not be identified by either the tasters or the experimenters themselves. This type of trial is known as a 'double blind', when no one knows which food is which.

The method used was 'triangular testing' whereby the tasters were given three samples, two of which were the same. The tasters first have to pick the odd one out, and then have to say which they prefer.

With the oranges, three out of eight tasters chose the wrong one – they selected one of a pair of the same oranges as the odd one out. Of the five who chose correctly, three preferred the organically grown oranges. A total of three out of eight.

The chickens were roasted and this time only two out of eight correctly identified the odd one out. Of these two, one preferred the free-range chicken.

All the tasters correctly identified the odd one out amongst the jams. Seven out of eight preferred the organically fertilized raspberry jam, five out of eight preferred the organically fertilized blackcurrant jam.

The BBC 'Today' programme conducted a small trial on eggs in February 1964. At that time, ordinary eggs bore a Lion stamp, and their flavour was compared with farm eggs, without the stamp, that cost more and were said to be superior. George Villers on the programme 'Shopping List' said that he could not taste any difference, and four listeners who said they could were put to the test. Two men and two women were given four eggs (boiled for 4½ minutes), a glass of water and some plain bread. One of each four eggs was an unstamped free-range egg which had cost twice as much as the ordinary egg.

In the first round of tasting, three panellists selected the ordinary egg. In the second round, the score was two-two. The test was repeated with fried eggs and the score was again two-two. One man was able to pick the free-range egg every time.

Anglia TV conducted a similar experiment in September 1963 when four out of five tasters chose battery eggs. The Egg Marketing Board conducted five tests in November 1959 with six tasters. Three free-range, one deep-litter and one battery egg were used. One person selected two out of the five correctly, one selected one of the five and the others could not tell any difference at all.

The Food Science Department of the University of Florida conducted one of the few thorough and detailed taste trials reported (*Journal of Milk Food Technology, Vol. 37, 1974*). Twenty-five foods were purchased in both health and ordinary shops. In some cases, the same food was bought in two health food shops or two ordinary shops. The food from the traditional shops was mass-produced, packaged, coloured, flavoured and, where necessary, preserved.

Twenty men and women aged between 18 and 60 met three or four times a week over a period of three months to give their opinion on colour, flavour, texture and odour. They also gave their opinions on 'overall acceptability'. They were asked to mark the food on a scale of 1 to 9, with 1 being 'dislike extremely' and 9 meaning 'like extremely'.

Not one single 'health food' was deemed superior to the ordinary food in 'overall acceptance'. Ten ordinary foods, however, were preferred overall – dried apples, apple juice, apple sauce, cashew nuts, Swiss cheese, coconut, ice cream, mayonnaise with tomato, peanut butter and sesame chips with tomato juice. In many cases no differences whatsoever were detected.

VALUE FOR MONEY

Most of us are influenced by price. Anything – not just food – that costs more 'must' be better than the cheaper version. Ordinary food sold in health food shops usually costs more than it would in the supermarket, thus persuading many people that it is in some way better.

I have made price comparisons over a number of years to avoid problems such as special reductions which would bias the results. In 1977 some health food shops in London were charging 25 per cent more than ordinary shops for brown rice, lentils and wholemeal flour; dried apricots were 62 per cent more and clover honey was 120 per cent more – over twice the price!

Even meat, lamb cutlets, ox liver, beef and steak were between 10 per cent and 37 per cent dearer; Muscovado (brown) sugar was 40 per cent and Demerara 52 per cent dearer. Cottage cheese, butter and bran were, respectively, 17 per cent, 23 per cent and 25 per cent dearer than in the ordinary shop! Sea salt, an impure form of salt, was two and a quarter times as expensive as ordinary (pure) salt.

Some mass-produced, branded foods are available in both health food and ordinary shops. The same brand of treacle cost 15 per cent more in the health food shop; 100 per cent organically grown flour in the same miller's packaging cost 7 per cent more; the wheat germ preparation Bemax was 15 per cent dearer and 'pure thick honey' cost 28 per cent more for the same brand in the health food shop.

That was in 1977. When comparing prices in a different part of London in 1978, skim milk powder was just twice the price of a nationally advertised brand. In another part of London in 1982, the same brand of margarine sold for 38p in a health food shop and 30p in a supermarket a few hundred yards away. One nationally advertised brand of breakfast cereal cost 81p

Taste panel's evaluation of Health Foods v Traditional Foods

Points scored out of 9 (two different samples of some foods were tested)

Product		Odour	Colour	Texture	Flavour	Overall acceptance	cost/oz U.S. Dollars
Apple juice	Traditional	7.2	7.0	7.4	7.2	7.4	$ .012
	Health	6.0	3.8	4.3	4.6	4.2	.033
	Health	6.6	5.1	5.9	6.0	5.6	.028
Beans/	Traditional	7.0	7.4	7.3	7.2	7.2	.015
tomato sauce	Health	7.2	7.3	7.4	6.7	6.8	.023
Bread	Traditional	7.2	6.9	6.8	6.9	6.9	.028
whole wheat	Health	6.9	7.4	6.8	6.9	7.1	.031
	Traditional	7.0	7.4	7.5	7.0	7.2	.024
Cereal	Traditional	7.0	6.8	5.6	7.1	7.1	.041
	Health	5.3	6.2	5.4	5.5	5.9	.049
Mild Cheddar	Health	6.5	5.1	6.5	6.8	6.7	.120
cheese	Traditional	6.2	7.5	6.7	6.5	6.8	.076
	Traditional	5.8	7.1	7.0	6.4	6.6	.085
Fig bars	Health	7.0	6.5	7.0	7.0	7.0	.044
	Traditional	7.8	7.4	7.0	7.2	7.4	.044
	Traditional	6.2	7.0	6.2	6.7	6.6	.022
Orange	Traditional	6.2	8.4	7.4	6.8	7.0	.043
blossom honey	Health	6.3	7.0	7.2	6.2	6.8	.056
	Traditional	6.8	7.2	7.5	7.2	7.4	.042
Ice cream	Health	6.2	6.6	7.5	6.7	6.7	.035
	Traditional	7.6	7.9	8.2	8.3	8.4	.015
Ketchup	Health	7.0	7.9	7.6	7.7	7.6	.016
	Traditional	7.2	7.0	7.0	7.4	7.2	.024
Peanut butter	Health	6.6	6.1	4.2	5.3	4.8	.040
	Traditional	7.7	7.3	7.4	7.3	7.2	.040
	Health	6.4	5.8	4.5	3.9	4.0	.095
	Traditional	6.9	7.7	7.6	6.3	6.4	.040
Rice	Health	6.8	5.4	5.5	5.9	5.9	.026
long grain	Traditional	7.1	7.0	7.0	6.0	6.2	.026
Tomato juice	Traditional	7.4	7.4	6.9	7.1	7.2	.093
	Health	5.4	5.8	5.8	2.8	3.0	.225

compared with 69p in an ordinary shop; another cereal made by the same manufacturer cost 67p compared with the ordinary price of 51p. Shoppers could choose from three brands of sunflower oil: the supermarket 'own brand' at 75p per litre, a named brand at £1.14 or the 'health food' oil at £1.59.

Out of the twenty-five foods tasted in the Florida research laboratories described earlier, twenty cost more from the health food shops.

In June 1978 *Which?* compared prices in 79 health food and 31 wholefood shops with prices in the major supermarket chains. They examined a total of 132 foods. Fifteen brands available in both health food shops and supermarkets were consistently higher priced in the former. Flour and cereals were generally 5 per cent higher, while mineral waters, dates and some treacles and sugars cost as much as 15–20 per cent more.

The article did point out that since health food shops are closer in size to the corner grocery shop than the supermarket, the consumer should expect to pay more. What it did not take into account was its own statement that one sixth of all health food shops (in 1978) were owned by a single large chain. In their case, it should have been possible to buy in large quantities. Since then many more health food shops have been franchised by chains so that they should all be obtaining their branded goods in larger, and therefore cheaper, quantities than the small shopkeeper.

Which? examined branded goods sold mainly in health food shops and found them generally more expensive than similar unbranded products sold in health food, wholefood or other shops. So a higher price does not buy better nutrition or guarantee better flavour. Perhaps it just buys hope.

THE ORGANIC FARMER

An interesting light was thrown on this area of discussion in a series of broadcasts during July and August 1984 on the BBC early morning farming programme.

The arguments in favour of organic farming fell under four headings.

1. Sustainability – meaning that the ordinary farm relying on fertilizers and chemical sprays will break down when such aids are discontinued, while production based on growing cereals/legumes/animals can continue indefinitely.

2. Quality. This was defined simply as freedom from contaminants.

3. Efficiency. It was agreed that without the use of fertilizers the yield of food would fall but this would even be an advantage in the Common Market where too much food is being produced. Further, since it requires more labour, organic farming would make a contribution towards solving the problems of the unemployed.

4. Price. It was agreed that with this low productivity and higher labour costs, despite the saving on chemical aids, food would cost more. This, however, was quite all right because the consumers are willing to pay more for what was termed freedom from nitrates (but all plants contain nitrates) and chemicals.

The listener was left with the impression that organic farming was a good thing so long as there were sufficient customers to pay up.

It was suggested that the alternative to reducing efficiency of production by ceasing to use chemical aids was to reduce the price paid to farmers who would then produce less.

The argument used against chemical aids was mainly that the Government had vested interests in the fertilizer industry and so the discussion was all about politics and money and had nothing to do with nutrition and health.

LONG LIFE

One hope that we buy in the health food shop is for longer life. There are many stories of people living to extraordinary ages, invariably in remote areas of the world and invariably on mystical, magical foods. One such story is found in an old textbook which maintains that Bulgarian peasants live to be 107 (unexpectedly precise data) because they eat yoghurt. At the time that book was written, yoghurt was an unusual food.

Fo-Tieng is a herbal mixture claimed to have 'a marvellous rejuvenating effect on the brain cells and endocrine glands.' It was discovered, it is claimed, by Professor Yun, a Chinese herbalist who died in 1933 at the age of 256. *The Guinness Book of Records* is offered as evidence for this but that book simply states that this claim has been made and does not provide any further 'evidence'.

Stories of long life surface regularly in newspapers and occasionally in scientific literature. It is rumoured that people live to be over 100 years old in the Hunza Valley in India, in Georgia in Russia, in Vermont in the United States and in various remote parts of South America and the rest of the world. Invariably the tellers of these tales conclude that 'it must be due to their diet'.

If this were indeed the case, it would still be impossible to prove. If very old people were found in different places eating foods unknown to us, what could we look for? How can we analyse a food if we don't know what to look for? And how long should a lifetime experiment be continued?

In fact these groups of people do not exist. The closest claim came in 1973 when a zoologist from University College in London found 'proof' in a community in Vilcabamba in Ecuador. The villagers there had baptismal certificates showing that many were 150 years old. This was the first documentary – as opposed to hearsay – evidence ever produced (*New Scientist, 2 February 1973*). The scientist was convinced their longevity 'must be due to the food' and tried to persuade nutritionists to investigate. It later transpired that the baptismal certificates belonged to the villagers' parents!

Dr. R. E. Hughes in his book *Vitamin C – Some Current Problems,* uncritically quotes Russian authorities regarding the life-lengthening properties of large doses of vitamin C. He says (p. 62): 'Belief in the "life-extending" properties of ascorbic acid crops up in all sorts of places. A report from Russia [a reference is given to *Voprosy Pitaniya, Vol. 32, pp.*

27-31, 1973 abstracted in English in Nutrition Abstracts and Reviews 1974, Vol. 4, p. 860] indicated that in Dagestan the long-lived inhabitants of the mountains (the maximum life span there in 1973 was 116) had an ascorbic acid intake some ten times greater than that of the shorter-living occupants of the plains ... Dr. Linus Pauling, in the preface to the most recent edition of his *apologia for megatherapy* has expressed the belief that for most people sustained ascorbic acid supplementation would increase the life-span by twelve to eighteen years (a threefold increase on the first edition estimate).' *(A Physician's Handbook on Orthomolecular Medicine)*

It would appear from the phrase in brackets that the author is somewhat sceptical of Pauling's claims. Short of conducting a lifetime experiment on large numbers of people living under identical conditions (in itself impossible to achieve) it would be impossible to demonstrate that vitamin C makes people live longer.

Any nutritionist who might be tempted to investigate the diets of long-living groups would find numerous complications. In Vilcabamba for instance meals were described as 'frugal', consisting as they did of only 1200–1300 Calories daily, but the populace tended to smoke 40–60 cigarettes each day and consume regular quantities of home-made rum! On the other hand, the Georgians of the USSR have an abundant diet of wheat, corn, fish, game and beans, plus a wide range of fruits with, of course, yoghurt.

In addition to special diets, individual foods are often claimed to have special properties. One of the most thoroughly recommended foods is brown rice. Fostered by the followers of the Zen macrobiotic diet, brown rice was particularly praised during the Vietnam war when we were told that the Viet Cong owed their success to 'a handful of roasted rice every day' – as if anything else was unnecessary. Some manufacturers also maintain that the Viet Cong 'rushed into battle against the Americans armed with ginseng'.

'Many Soviet health authorities' have attributed the Georgians' alleged tendency towards long life to buttermilk and pickled vegetables 'which destroy the harmful bacteria in the intestine and prevent development of hardening of the arteries'. The Iroquois Indians are said to owe their health to a soup made from the excrement of deer! California Indians can march for twenty-four hours on just one teaspoon of a seed called Chia (Salvia columbariae). It is of course quite possible to walk for that length of time without any food at all – political protesters and professional fasters have lived for weeks without eating.

Cooking Naturally for Pleasure and Health informs us that in a yogic diet air, when consumed properly, is the highest food. Well-trained yogis can live for a week – or even months – on nothing but special breathing techniques. Even the authors appear to consider this far-fetched because they continue: 'These are the fabled, but rarely encountered, breatharians.'

Taken alone, any of these claims might sound feasible. Shown side by side they become a matter of 'believe it or not'.

The manner in which people begin to believe their own stories was demonstrated in *The Times* (4 February 1984).

> *'One day I read an article which claimed that the British government was flying prostitutes into the RAF base which lay to the west of the capital, the object being to infiltrate them into Baghdad where they would corrupt the morals and physical well-being of the Iraqi youth. I met the editor, whom I knew, a few days later. I said that we did not particularly mind being criticized or even attacked. But did he not think that this article was a little extravagant, verging on an infringement of the offside rule?*
>
> *'He laughed and admitted that he and his staff had invented it. Then he paused and added: "Yet, you know, many of my readers believe it, so perhaps there is some truth in it after all."'*

EVIDENCE OR OLD WIVES' TALES?

Health food promoters complain because scientists do not accept their stories and demand evidence. Of course we do.

Anyone can make a statement or claim without offering evidence of its truth.

Evidence, to a scientist, means that a verifiable report of the work has been published in a reputable scientific journal which, in turn, means that it has been examined by referees and the editor for reliability, accuracy and acceptable conclusions – a process sometimes called 'peer review'. It is also preferable that other workers report similar findings so that the evidence becomes strong enough to be established as fact.

Old wives' tales on the other hand are just tales. One leaflet from health food salesmen complains that scientists do not accept anecdotes as evidence. Certainly we do not believe that toast makes the hair curl, or that fish make brains or that brown eggs are nutritionally superior to white – all old wives' tales and all untrue. Your hair will curl if you are born with curly hair (or go to the hairdresser). Brain development and function do not require foods other than those required by the rest of the body and no individual food is particularly recommended for improving brain power. Brown eggs are exactly the same as white except for the colour of the shell.

Nor do we accept statements as true because 'everybody knows'. Once upon a time 'everybody' knew that the earth was flat.

Unusual, dramatic and sensational statements are considered newsworthy. Cancer scares about green pea dye or claims that vitamin X can increase sexual potency make headlines, but statements that fish and chips and baked beans on toast are good food do not. They are not sufficiently dramatic. So the unusual and unexpected are widely broadcast on radio and television and in the newspapers. It is left to more serious-minded people to pick up the pieces and rectify any damage that has resulted or to replace public misinformation with correct information. Unfortunately the truth does not often catch up with the lie.

Hence reputable scientists require evidence. And the kind of evidence offered by health food salesmen is usually nothing more than stories from people providing testimonials that certain foods or pills have cured them.

Natural Choice No. 17, a leaflet on garlic produced by Holland and Barrett, states that 'most of garlic's reputation is based firmly on centuries of experience, relayed from person to person, as well as recorded by doctors and herbalists. People who've found it seemed to shift their clogged catarrh, or who found that the winter they took garlic was the one winter they were never ill, tell their friends – and so the word spreads.' Such relaying of 'information' carries no weight with the scientific community.

Another unacceptable statement is offered by Pearse in *Just Consequences (ed. R. Waller, Charles Knight, London, p. 72):* 'In this *anecdote* there is incontrovertible *evidence . . .*' The italics are mine. Later in this same book (p. 172) Mr. A. H. Walters writes: 'While engaged on a haematological investigation in a maternity hospital I observed that in a series of 2000 patients many women who had subsisted mainly on forced-fertilized and variously processed or frozen foods showed an increased incidence of anaemia during their pregnancy ... diminished blood serum iron, vitamin B12 and folic acid levels.' Figures relating to the groups of women are absent, as are details of the increased incidence compared, presumably, with women who do not eat 'forced-fertilized' and frozen foods. In fact, as I explained earlier, the type of fertilizer used has no effect on the nutritional value of food, but only on the plant's yield. Manure and compost generally improve the texture and water-holding properties of the soil, while inorganic fertilizers increase the nutrients the plant needs, and so increase the yield.

Apart from often being incorrect, anecdotes are quoted as if they are proven facts and the invention of a term such as 'forced-fertilized' is calculated to throw a scare into the reader.

5

OLD WIVES' TALES
TRUE OR FALSE?

Do carrots help you to see in the dark?
If you are short of vitamin A – which is very unusual in the
Western world – you do not see well in dim light (no one can
see in complete darkness). Carrots contain carotene which is
changed to vitamin A in the body, so it is true to say that *if* you
were short of vitamin A then carrots would enable you to see
better in dim light. If you have enough, more does not help.

Does vitamin A help poor eyesight?
No, poor eyesight, which is helped by wearing eyeglasses, has
nothing to do with nutrition. The error arose years ago when it
was found that vitamin A was part of the mechanism of seeing
in dim light (see previous question). This was misunderstood
by some advertisers who claimed that it helped poor eyesight.
The mistake is still seen in some advertisements.

Is it true that an apple a day keeps the doctor away?
Apples may be attractive, but they are not particularly
nutritious. Nor do they provide any special immunity from
illness. A medium-sized apple of say 4 oz contains only 5–10
mg of vitamin C and small traces of other vitamins, no protein
worth speaking of and approximately 50 Calories. As fruits go
it has a moderate amount of dietary fibre – approximately 2 g.

Does spinach make you strong?
No more than some other dark green vegetables. It is rich in
carotene, but not more than watercress, moderate in vitamin C

131

and rich in iron but not as good as Popeye led us to believe. More surprising, spinach contains a lot of protein for a vegetable – 5 g of protein per 100 g portion – which is more than you would get from corn on the cob and as much as baked beans. Compare this with cabbage and watercress which have 2 per cent protein. Perhaps the bigger surprise is that on the plate baked beans at 5 per cent protein and maize at 4 per cent protein have less than white bread which has 7.8 per cent protein. This mistake comes from people who look at food composition tables and see 'beans, haricot, raw – 21.4 per cent protein' (compare this with meat at 20–25 per cent). But we do not eat raw, dried beans. When they are cooked, beans take up more than three times their weight in water. So cooked beans have only 6.6 per cent protein and canned baked beans in tomato sauce just 5 per cent.

Does eating onions prevent colds?
No.

Do peanuts make you sexy?
No. This one is probably a *young* wives' tale.

Does beetroot juice help to prevent anaemia?
No. This belief started because beetroot juice is the same colour as blood, but they are quite different.

Is brown bread better than white?
Yes. Wholemeal bread contains more of the B vitamins and iron, and a little more protein, than white bread. Brown breads fall between the two.

More important, perhaps, wholemeal bread contains 9 per cent dietary fibre compared with 4 per cent in white bread. The germ and outer bran are removed when wheat is milled to make white flour and that is where the nutrients are partially lost.

Are brown eggs better than white eggs?
No. The colour of the shell does not reflect any difference at all

in the nutrients in an egg. They sometimes cost more for two reasons. First, the kind of chicken that lays brown eggs lays fewer than the other kind. Secondly, if there is a demand for brown eggs, then shops can charge more.

Is brown sugar better than white?
Apart from the very dark brown sugars, there is no difference at all (see p. 103). The darkest sugar contains about 0.7 mg of iron and 10 mg of calcium per ounce, an insignificant amount. There is no iron or calcium at all in white sugar.

Are deep-coloured egg yolks better than light yolks?
Yes but only for vitamin A. There is no difference at all in protein or other vitamins.

Why is honey special?
It isn't. It consists only of sugars – glucose and fructose – and about one quarter water. There are traces of nutrients but they are too slight to be of any use in the diet (see page 75).

Does honey help you sleep?
No. It has no effect other than providing energy in the form of sugar. There are just under 3 Calories per gram, about the same as in jam, compared with 4 Calories per gram in sugar (which does not contain any water).

Does yoghurt help you slim?
All foods are fattening if you eat enough of them. Yoghurt is nutritionally similar to the milk from which it is made. There are low-fat yoghurts which are slightly lower in calories and, of course, in fats. It can be only be regarded as helpful on a reducing diet if eaten instead of more calorific foods.

Is natural yoghurt better than fruit-flavoured yoghurt?
The term 'natural' tends to be used for unsweetened yoghurt, compared with fruit yoghurts which are generally sweetened with sugar, so in this sense it is better.

Is live yoghurt particularly good?

No. Most yoghurts are pasteurized and bacteria killed off, otherwise the yoghurt would change in its container. Live yoghurts are quite safe to eat because any harmful bacteria present in the milk are swamped by the souring bacteria, but they are no better nutritionally than ordinary pasteurized yoghurt. The idea that the bacteria in live yoghurt can flourish in the human intestine and that they are beneficial is very questionable.

Is margarine less fattening than butter?

No. They both contain 85 per cent fat and an equal number of calories.

Is fish good for the brain?

Unfortunately no single food is good for the brain. There is no food or dietary supplement that will help either to develop the brain or improve the memory.

Does coffee keep you awake?

Some people cannot sleep after consuming caffeine, and some suffer more after drinking coffee than tea, which also contains caffeine. Other people are not affected by a cup of coffee last thing at night.

Does coffee help you sober up after drinking alcohol?

No.

Is it bad to give tea and coffee to small children?

Generally speaking, drugs and stimulants of any kind – including those in tea and coffee – should not be given to children.

Why is 'a nice cup of tea' so refreshing and stimulating?

Partly because it contains caffeine, partly because it is a hot drink and partly because we associate tea with comfort and sympathy.

Should you put milk in the cup before or after the tea?
The only difference is that if the milk is put in afterwards the tannins in the tea might stain the cup and if the milk is put in first the tannins are precipitated. Otherwise, taste it and see if you prefer one way to the other.

Is lemon juice good for slimming?
It has no effect. It used to be thought by some people that it helps because it is sour and some people even thought that lemon juice shrinks the stomach, but it doesn't.

Is it true that sugar is essential for energy?
No. We get energy from all our foods. Sugar is not essential to anyone's diet.

Is it true that you must eat meat for strength?
No. Many people live very well on purely vegetable diets. Meat is by no means essential.

Are all sweet foods fattening?
Sweet foods generally contain a lot of sugar – unless artificial sweeteners are used – and are therefore higher in calories than foods that are not sweet. Furthermore, if you like sweet things, you tend to eat a lot of them and it is the quantity that is fattening.

Are artificial sweeteners safe?
Yes. Saccharine, aspartame and acesulphame, among others, have been thoroughly tested and shown to be safe. Even cyclamate, which is not allowed in some countries, has not been shown to be harmful to human beings.

Why mustn't diabetics eat sugar?
They cannot metabolize sugar properly thus causing the blood sugar, glucose, to increase too much and some comes out in the urine. They must avoid eating sugar and foods containing sugar. They do seem able to deal with the fructose and glucose present in fruit adequately if eaten in reasonable amounts.

Does grapefruit burn off fat?

No. The so-called grapefuit diet was just a gimmick to help sell grapefruits. There is no food that helps to burn off fat or other foods.

What about the potato and banana diets?

These allowed you to eat as many potatoes or bananas as you liked, but how many would you want to eat? The diets were so monotonous that people didn't eat very much and those who persisted in following the diet did lose weight, but most people gave up after just a day or two.

Are bananas fattening?

Bananas are 20 per cent sugar, so they contain more calories than most other fruit. In terms of calories per mouthful, then, they are fattening. Most fruit and vegetables contain much more water than do bananas.

Are fat people jolly?

Very fat people are usually unhappy because they are the object of ridicule and they often prefer to avoid other people.

Is toast less fattening than bread?

No. A slice of bread is a slice of bread whether toasted or not and has the same calorific value either way. The toast will weigh less only because it has lost some water in the toasting.

Is white wine better than red when slimming?

Red and white wine both supply 70 Calories per 3½ oz glass if dry, increasing to 80 Calories in medium and 90 Calories in sweet wine. The sweeter the wine, the more sugar it contains. So any wine should be taken in small amounts only – or not at all – if you are trying to lose weight.

Should you drink less when slimming?

No. Water, or any drink, is essential for the body and if you drink more than you need the body soon gets rid of it. What goes in goes out. If you severely restricted your fluid intake you would lose weight by dehydration – loss of body fluid – which is very dangerous. Your body will not retain any more liquid than it needs, no matter how much you drink. Oedema is too much retention and needs medical treatment, but it does not occur just from drinking too much. It is the consumption of sweetened drinks which adds calories.

Am I fat because of my glands?
The only glands involved, it is sometimes said, are the salivary glands. Glandular diseases causing obesity are very, very rare and even when they occur, the fat person is eating more calories than he or she is using.

Am I overweight because I have heavy bones?
While it is true that a person with a heavy frame (large skeleton) will normally weigh more than one with a light frame, bones, as such, do not weigh any more than flesh and fat. Most people who say they have heavy bones are just offering an excuse. This is well expressed by the saying 'I am not too fat for my height but too short for my weight'.

Does red meat cause gout?
No. It was once thought that port and red meat caused gout because it seemed to be more common amongst rich, elderly men who consumed large quantities of both. White meat does not really differ from red and the cause of gout is still unclear.

Are acid fruits like lemons and rhubarb bad for rheumatism?
No. Rheumatism is not affected by diet. Nor do acid fruits cause acidity in the tissues (see p. 56). Acid fruits contain citric and other acids and also sodium citrate. The acidic part of the citric acid and the citrate are burned completely in the body to carbon dioxide and water and the alkaline sodium is left.

Is yellow butter better than pale butter?
If the colour comes naturally from the grass the cows ate then it is carotene and the butter will be richer in vitamin A. Some

butter is coloured artificially, however, and in that case colour is no guide at all.

Is the vitamin C from fruit still present in jam?
Very, very little. Jam is 67 per cent sugar in any case.

Are artificial colours harmful?
So far as we know, none of the food additives – colours, flavours, preservatives and the rest – are harmful, otherwise they would not be permitted in food.

Is milk bad for adults?
On the contrary, milk is a good food for everyone. It is rich in protein, vitamins A and B2, calcium and many other nutrients in small amounts. Only the fat might be harmful but that is because we eat too much fat anyway (see Chapter 8).

Do you have to drink six glasses of water a day?
Your own thirst will tell you how much to drink. You do not need to make any special effort to drink.

Is chlorinated water harmful?
No. Treatment with chlorine kills off bacteria and makes the water safe to drink, although it sometimes gives it an unpleasant taste.

Must we eat breakfast?
Nutritionally it is best to have three regular meals daily, but many people just cannot stand eating breakfast and it does not seem to do them any harm.

Do peas cause flatulence?
In many people peas and beans do cause flatulence – as do other foods. It varies from person to person and time to time; you can usually find out for yourself which foods do not agree with you and how many peas or beans you can tolerate.

Is soya meat substitute as good as meat?
Nutritionally it is about the same because manufacturers usually add the main nutrients that are present in meat, i.e. vitamins B1, B12 and iron. Meat does contain other nutrients, but since most vegetarians are perfectly healthy, it would seem that meat is not essential to the diet. As regards taste, most people prefer meat to any substitute.

Can a glass of milk taken before you start drinking alcohol stop you getting drunk?
You can get drunk very quickly on an empty stomach because the alcohol is quickly absorbed into the bloodstream. If there is food in the stomach, particularly fatty food, the alcohol stays there longer and is absorbed more slowly, so a glass of milk can be a help.

Do apples clean your teeth?
Yes. The crispness of the apple helps to remove sticky sugars and also makes the saliva flow thus washing the sugars off the teeth.

Why do sweets cause tooth decay?
All fermentable carbohydrates can form acid on the teeth and attack them, but sugar is worse than fruit sugars and starch. It is the frequency of eating sweets that really causes the problem because the teeth are then continuously bathed in sugar and exposed to the acid that is formed.

Is vitamin E good for sex?
Only for rats and mice.

Do 'nightcaps' help you to sleep?
Any hot drink before going to bed helps some people, but not everyone. Some of the proprietary night drinks have been shown to reduce restlessness and so help people to sleep but the evidence has not been properly confirmed. Try it for yourself – you might be lucky.

Does drinking water with a meal dilute the digestive juices and slow down the digestion?
No. The fluid passes around the wall of the stomach and leaves without mixing with the food already there.

Does smoking after a meal help digestion?
No. Smoking does not help anything. On the contrary, it is always harmful.

Are walnuts good for the brain?
No. This myth arose from the similarity in appearance between the walnut and the brain. There is no truth in it.

Are oysters good for sex?
No. This one is an old husbands' tale.

Does alcohol help your appetite?
Yes. An aperitif or any (small) alcoholic drink about a quarter of an hour before a meal stimulates the flow of gastric juices and also the appetite. Too much may put you off the idea of eating at all.

Does a pregnant woman have to eat for two?
No. We used to think that a pregnant woman should eat for one and a quarter – after all the embryo is very small – but recent research has shown that women do not need any more food during pregnancy because their bodies adapt to the extra needs of the baby and they make more efficient use of the food. However, since any slight deficiency of a vitamin or mineral that might not affect an adult can affect a baby in the womb, it is very important that enough vitamins and minerals are taken throughout pregnancy.

Are proteins good on a slimming diet?
All food is fattening if you eat enough of it. Protein supplies the same 4 Calories per gram as carbohydrates. But a protein-rich diet might be a help in slimming because foods like meat and cheese are very filling and stay in the stomach longer than straight carbohydrates, so you actually eat less.

6

VITAMIN MAGIC

Vitamins have always been with us, but the word itself was not coined until 1912. Although Sylvester Graham did not really know what Adam and Eve ate (see p. 18), we can be certain that their diet included vitamins for they could not, indeed, have lived without them.

WHY DO WE NEED THEM?

Vitamins play a part in almost every metabolic process – to help to release the energy from food, to build up and repair tissues and to keep the organs functioning. No one can live if any vitamin is missing from the diet. If one is in short supply, the result is ill-health.

Vitamins can be compared with the lubricating oil of a motor-car engine. If the calcium phosphate skeleton of the body and its clothing of flesh are regarded as the bodywork of the car, and the muscles as the engine, then fats and carbohydrates (and protein in excess of body building needs) are the fuel. Muscles burn up food to supply energy just as a car burns petrol. But the engine cannot function without oil. Although it is only needed in small amounts, it is absolutely essential. Compared with petrol, very little oil is lost from the engine. We use gallons of petrol every week but only a pint of oil every month or so. Similarly, very small amounts of vitamins are used up so we need amounts measured in milligrams and micrograms compared with tens and hundreds of grams of carbohydrates, fats and proteins.

A LITTLE OR A LOT?

You can see food – bread, meat, potatoes or cornflakes – but you cannot see the proteins, the carbohydrates, the vitamins and the minerals – the nutrients in the food. They are part of the food. A loaf of bread looks like a homogeneous white or brown sponge, but it is made of carbohydrates, proteins, fat, vitamins and mineral salts plus other substances that give it colour, flavour and smell. It also contains approximately 40 per cent water.

The only way to see these nutrients is to separate them in the laboratory. One hundred grams of white bread ($3\frac{1}{2}$ oz) can be separated into its constituents – not flour, yeast, salt and water, but carbohydrate, protein and other nutrients. We would then have 47 g of starch, 7.8 g of protein, 4 g of dietary fibre and 1.7 g of fat. The remaining nutrients are present, apart from 1.5 g of salt, in such small quantities that they are measured in milligrams, not grams – 100 mg potassium, 100 mg calcium, 26 mg magnesium, 97 mg phosphorus, 1.7 mg iron, 0.8 mg zinc and 0.15 mg copper.

Then we come to the vitamins, some measurable in milligrams but others in even smaller microgram quantities (one thousandth part of a milligram which is itself one thousandth part of a gram). Our 100 g of bread contains vitamin B1, 0.18 mg; B2, 0.03 mg; niacin, 1.4 mg; B6, 0.04 mg; pantothenic acid, 0.3 mg; folic acid, 2.7 micrograms and biotin (vitamin H), 1 microgram. (Bread does not contain any vitamin A, C, D or B12.)

Once these vitamins have been extracted from the bread you can see them – even if the micrograms of some of the vitamins may be hard to see. You can, of course, see and handle all these vitamins when they are produced in quantity in the factory – whether by extraction from foods or synthesized.

When we are told that 100 grams of bread contains so many milligrams or micrograms of a mineral salt or a vitamin, the question is 'is this a little or a lot?'

Most of us eat 2–2.5 lb (about 1 kg) of food daily, half of which is made up of water. So are the few milligrams and micrograms of vitamins in a loaf of bread a little or a lot? Does wholemeal bread contain *only* 0.26 mg of thiamin, or does it contain *as much as* 0.26 mg? Note the way in which cunning wording can be used to mislead us.

To find the answer, we would have to compare the nutrients in that loaf of bread with the amounts of each nutrient which we need to eat. While each individual is different, we do know what the average person needs. This figure, plus a safety margin of 20 per cent, is known as the recommended daily amount or allowance (RDA). So we can recalculate the amount of nutrients in 100 g of bread – about three slices (without butter or jam) – as the proportion of the recommended daily amount of each nutrient that they will provide:

	Recommended daily amount for an adult man	Per cent of RDA in 100 g of wholemeal bread
Vitamin A	750 micrograms	None
B1	1.2 milligrams	22 per cent
B2	1.7 mg	5 per cent
Niacin	18 mg	22 per cent
Vitamin C	30 mg	None
D	2.5 micrograms	None
B6*	2 mg	7 per cent
B12*	3 micrograms	None
E*	400 mg	0.05 per cent

*The British authorities do not believe that we have enough knowledge to set a figure for the RDA but say that if we eat the foods that would supply enough of the vitamins for which we do have such information, we would most likely obtain enough of the other vitamins. The American authorities have no such inhibitions, and the RDAs given above for vitamins B6, B12 and E are taken from American tables.

Thus three slices of bread provide one fifth of our daily needs of vitamin B1 and niacin and can be regarded as a very good source of these vitamins. They are also a useful, but lesser, source of vitamins B2 and B6.

143

THE DISCOVERY OF VITAMINS

Two lines of investigation – the observation of human diseases and laboratory experiments with animals – led to the discovery of vitamins late in the nineteenth and early in the twentieth century.

Captain Lind of the British Navy effected the first cure of a disease with food in 1752. Scurvy had wiped out entire ships' crews over the centuries and although it was suspected that diet was its cause, the facts were not clear. Hippocrates described scurvy as early as 450 B.C. When the Portuguese explorer Vasco de Gama sailed around the Cape of Good Hope from Europe in 1479, two thirds of his crew died of scurvy. The explorer Cartier spent the winter of 1535 in Canada and was shown by the Indians how to prevent scurvy with a brew of spruce needles. We now know that vitamin C is provided by fruit and vegetables, but before the days of canning and freezing, there was no way of preserving them. When sailors were away from land for long periods, they could not, therefore, obtain these foods. Scurvy was also common in late winter in Northern Europe where fruit and vegetables were scarce.

Captain Lind, Physician to the Fleet, conducted an experiment at sea. Six pairs of sailors with scurvy were each given one of the treatments then thought to be useful (vinegar, a dilute solution of sulphuric acid and a variety of drugs) but only those given an orange or lemon recovered. It was then realized that something in the food cured the disease, but it took another 150 years before that 'something' was identified. After his experiment, though, the British Navy was protected with lime juice – hence the term 'Limeys' – and continues to be to this day. Scurvy largely disappeared by the end of the seventeenth century on land because new vegetable crops had been introduced.

There are other, similar, vitamin deficiency diseases. Thousands of people in the Far East died from beri-beri because their main food was white rice, which does not contain enough vitamin B1, and they did not have enough of the other foods which could supply it. As recently as the 1930s thousands of people in Italy and the southern U.S. died from pellagra – a deficiency of the vitamin called niacin.

The causes of these deficiency diseases gradually came to light when scientists tried to feed rats and mice on purified diets. The animals failed to grow – and would eventually have died – when given starch as their carbohydrate, fat, purified milk protein (casein) and mineral salts (which were already known to be essential in the diet). When small amounts of certain other foods were added to the diet the animals grew normally. This showed that something in the food, present in small amounts, was essential. Even half a teaspoon of milk made all the difference between a mouse growing or dying. And as I have explained, the fact that something is essential qualifies it as a vitamin.

The different vitamins were gradually discovered when the addition of one extracted vitamin concentrate failed to make the animals grow and another food was needed. In this way the first vitamin, appropriately called vitamin A, was distinguished from another, vitamin D, which was present alongside it in butter and cod liver oil. It was called D because vitamins B and C had meanwhile been discovered.

It is now possible to feed animals – and human beings – entirely on purified foodstuffs with the addition of thirteen vitamins and about twenty mineral salts. Astronauts in the early days of space experiments were able to live in this way. Hospital patients who have to be fed with a solution of nutrients directly into the veins can also be kept alive and recover from surgery or illness with a mixture of all the known nutrients.

When vitamins were first discovered, they had to be extracted from foods. Vitamin C came from fruit and in greater concentration from green peppers; vitamin B1 from rice bran and so on, because these were the foods that the researchers used as a good source of the then mysterious substance. Many of the B vitamins were found in yeast, vitamin E in pig fat and vitamin K was found by accident in fish meal that had gone bad (it was being produced in the fish meal by the bacteria growing in it).

Once nutritionists found that a particular food was a good source of a new nutrient, they worked with chemists to purify the extracted foodstuff. Eventually, often after years of work in numerous laboratories all over the world, a pure crystalline vitamin was produced. Chemists would then analyse the material and find out exactly what it was.

Vitamins vary from C (ascorbic acid), a small molecule chemically but not biologically related to glucose, to B12, a very large molecule related chemically to the structure of the red haemoglobin in blood and the green chlorophyll of plants. Chemical relations do not imply biological relations. One of the B vitamins, niacin, is also known as the pellagra-preventative vitamin, or PP. It is chemically related to nicotine but smoking, or even eating, cigarettes will not do you any good.

The final job of the chemists is to duplicate the molecule exactly, that is to synthesize the vitamin in a test tube. This is essential to ensure that what the chemists believe is the structure of the vitamin really is so. Nutritionists can then compare the extracted 'natural' vitamin with the synthetic one. Unless an absolutely identical effect can be produced, the chemists have not completed their work. If an identical effect can be produced, the vitamins can be made on a factory scale for treatment of the sick and undernourished and as a fortification for foods as a public health measure.

Vitamins synthesized in the factory are identical to those extracted from food. Vitamin C is vitamin C wherever it comes from – cabbage, blackcurrants or the chemist's shop. So claims for the superiority of vitamins extracted from food and called 'natural' are false.

There are six vitamins which are of particular nutritional importance because they are often in short supply in the diets of some communities – A, B1, B2, niacin, C and D. There are two others, B6 and folic acid, that may sometimes be in short supply, but we are not yet certain. In addition, there are seven that are never a dietary problem in any community – B12, biotin (vitamin H), vitamin K (except in rare medical

146

conditions), pantothenic acid, choline, inositol and para-amino benzoic acid. It is not clear whether these last three are vitamins (i.e. essential to the diet) for human beings or only experimental animals. Not included in any of these lists are the two non-existent vitamins on sale in health food shops, B15 and B17.

The function and main sources of the various vitamins are listed in the table and described in Chapter 8, What is a Healthy Diet? Each vitamin has a very specific function in the body and cannot be substituted. When we have to supply the body with fuel for energy, it does not matter whether we get the energy, i.e. calories, as carbohydrates, fats or proteins. Indeed the carbohydrates themselves can be sugars or starch. There are many types of sugar apart from the ordinary table variety as well as different types of starch in food. When it comes to vitamins, however, we need each one and there is no substitute, although some vitamins can be present in foods in slightly different chemical forms.

Vitamin A, for example, is found in animal foods such as liver and butter in a form called retinol. In plant foods it occurs in a form known as carotene. There are three forms of carotene commonly found in plant foods which are changed into retinol in the wall of the intestine before being absorbed into the blood so in fact the body can function with only the one substance, retinol. Vitamin B2 is found only as one form, riboflavin, and there is no substitute. Niacin is found as nicotinic acid and as nicotinamide, both of which are equally useful. Vitamin B6 is found in three different chemical forms and there are eight major forms of vitamin E with an even greater number of chemical variations on each.

The six vitamins of nutritional importance present public health problems in the sense that they are in short supply in diets in some parts of the world. Vitamin A and B2 (riboflavin) deficiencies present real problems in developing countries. It is estimated that some 60,000 children a year go blind in the south-east Pacific area from a deficiency of vitamin A. They do get a small amount, but not enough to maintain good health.

None of the other vitamins is ever in short supply unless the person is suffering from a particular illness or problem. For example, pernicious anaemia is due to a shortage of the blood-forming substances in the body, one of which is vitamin B12. Apart from very rare cases of vegans who may have diets deficient in this vitamin, pernicious anaemia is never caused by a dietary deficiency but by a disorder in which the person cannot absorb the vitamin from his food.

VITAMIN MAGIC

The effect of very small amounts of a vitamin in curing severe disease is dramatic. Beri-beri, caused by a shortage of B1, involves damage to the nerves resulting in paralysis of the legs, an enlarged heart and weak, wasted muscles. This horrifying catalogue of symptoms can be completely cured, or indeed prevented, by a few milligrams of B1 taken daily, a measure of how essential this vitamin is to health, and how little is needed.

If vitamins were discovered today with all the razzmatazz and hype of modern advertising, instead of in the 1920s and 1930s when it was still an infant art, it is easy to imagine what magical claims would be made for such miraculous substances. But are the claims made by health food shops for the virtues of vitamin supplements any less extravagant?

Health food fanatics are often carried away with the theories they have read or invented for themselves. One example is presented in a book by Doris Grant, *Your Daily Bread*. The book advocates using whole grain wheat flour which is certainly superior nutritionally to bread made with white flour. The author was so carried away with her own enthusiasm, though, that she put forward her own theory that unkneaded bread was superior to kneaded. This is not true. Mrs Grant suggested (and was modest enough to admit it is 'my own explanation of this, for what it is worth') that the air spaces formed in the dough by working the yeast may contain some of the essential oils, vitamins or other qualities of the wheat. When these air spaces are broken open during kneading, these qualities escape and are lost. 'I have had this theory confirmed recently by an old baker', she says, but he, too, was wrong.

Vitamins are solid substances in the wheat grain and are not volatile so could not possibly escape from the air spaces. The theory is totally untrue but sounds feasible to those who do not know the facts. It 'explains' something which is not true, that kneading dough reduces its nutritional value.

VITAMIN CLAIMS

Vitamins can be sold under licence according to the Medicines Act whereby the claims and amounts are controlled, or as foods subject only to the Labelling Regulations of the Ministry of Food. Those in health food shops are sold as food and claims and statements are less inhibited. The magazines and leaflets the shops distribute extol vitamins in articles not covered by any of the regulations or codes of practice that deal with advertisements and labels. Consequently they often imply that most of us will suffer from poor health because of a shortage of vitamins unless we buy their products. For example there is no shortage of vitamin B6 in the diets of Western Europe or North America – if indeed there is anywhere in the world – but it is highly acclaimed in countless health food shop supplements.

Sometimes manufacturers are more cautious in their wording. It is said, for instance, that 'many women prefer to take extra vitamin B6 prior to and during their periods and dosage can safely be increased at this time.'

A letter in the *Lancet (3 March 1984)* emphasized the difference between the food and medicine selling approaches. It stated that preparations marketed for medicinal purposes containing relatively high doses of folic acid are sold by pharmacists on prescription only, but that doses as high as 5 mg of folate and 25,000 international units of vitamin A – amounts that are potentially harmful – can be sold by mail order or over the counter as health foods.

Extravagant claims are made for chemicals that are not even

useful. The *1980 Report of the Food Standards Committee, Claims and Misleading Descriptions*, states that 'certain vitamins and minerals required by animals have not yet been demonstrated as being of use to the human body so they should be excluded from consideration in respect of claims for their presence in foods.'

In the 1972 Labelling of Food (Amendment) Regulations only vitamins A, B1, B2, niacin, C and D are scheduled – claims for others are prohibited, although they can be listed as ingredients. Health food shops get around all the regulations by promoting articles in magazines and free leaflets which make extravagant claims and then offering the products for sale.

As early as 1966 the Food Standards Committee recommended that no claims shall be made:

a that a full, properly mixed diet needs to be supplemented with vitamins;

b that good looks and good health in middle age or later can be maintained by vitamin products;

c that healthy people can be made to look younger or live longer by taking vitamin products;

d claims or implications that irritability, nerviness and lack of energy are only due to vitamin deficiency;

e that vitamins A, D or C hasten recovery from infections such as colds or influenza;

f that any additional benefit is obtained from a product containing more than 400 units (10 μg) vitamin D in a daily dose;

g that there is evidence of general and widespread vitamin deficiencies.

Claims **a**, **b**, **d** and **g** are unacceptable under the British Code in Advertising Practice. The remaining claims under **c** and **f** will probably be controlled under EEC Directives.

The health food industry manages to circumvent these 'undesirable claims' and at the same time to make claims for unscheduled nutrients – whether vitamins, mineral salts, enzymes and so-called biocatalysts together with a host of food extractives. It is permissible to make claims only for special categories of the population who either have greater needs than average or may be considered to be on a restricted diet. These include pregnant and nursing women, children, the elderly and those convalescing after illness. Legislation and the Code of Practice in Advertising only apply to claims made by salesmen, however, and cannot control what is written in articles and editorials. It is here that the health food movement goes overboard.

Miss Lee-Richardson, daughter of the 'leading, most powerful man in the trade' (according to the *Daily Telegraph Magazine 13 November 1970*) stated in 'Your Diet – Undeniable Evidence of Vitamin Deficiency', an article in *Here's Health*, that 'it (malnutrition) exists in babies, in children, in students, in industrial workers, in housewives, in the middle aged, in old people, in hospital patients, in all sections of the population'. The article consisted of extracts taken from a variety of research papers and reviews which made mention of any nutritional deficiency, any vitamin loss in cooking and any suggestion made by anyone that there might be a shortage in anyone's diet. The conclusion was that virtually everyone is short of vitamins and if it does not show it is simply because vitamin deficiencies take a long time to reveal themselves!

Vitamins are sold for everything from sexual stimulation to headaches. In *ASA Case Report 101 (September 1983)* a cure for a headache – 'Does thinking of ways to increase your profit give you a headache? If so, take these' – turned out to be vitamin C. In their defence the advertisers said they had consulted a pharmacist to find a pill that was totally harmless and had followed his advice to use vitamin C!

An advertisement for Vitasafeplan asked 'Do you wonder what makes you so darned tired? . . . It could well be that, in common with many other people your tiredness is due to a lack of vitamins and minerals in your diet.' The advertisement had to be withdrawn (*ASA Case Report 96, April 1983*).

BALANCED VITAMINS

Some of the products available in health food stores are labelled 'balanced vitamins'. These, according to the labels, are extracts of yeast or wheat germ and it is assumed that they supply the B vitamins in the right ratio for good health. But the right proportions for the wheat plant or yeast are not the same as the proportions needed by human beings.

In fact, we require about as much vitamin B1 as B2, and ten times as much niacin. Liver has ten times as much B2 as B1 and only five times as much niacin. If you ate 100 grams of raw liver or tablets made from dried liver, you would get twice as much B2 as you need for a day but only a fifth of the B1, a quarter of the B6 and enough B12 to last nearly a month. The niacin would be about right.

Bakers' yeast is more 'balanced' – you would need only 50 grams to provide the day's B1, B2 and niacin but this would provide only half the B6 and almost no vitamin B12 at all. Brewers' yeast, to complicate the picture, has seven times as much B1 as bakers' yeast.

The other rich source of B vitamins is wheat germ. 100 grams would provide exactly the amount of B1 you need for a day, but only half the B6, a third of the B2 and niacin and no B12 at all!

Amounts of B vitamins in 100 grams of food

	B1 mg	B2 mg	Niacin mg	B6 mg	B12 micrograms
raw calf liver	0.21	3.1	12.4	0.54	100
chicken liver	0.36	2.7	10.2	0.40	56
lamb liver	0.27	3.3	14.2	0.42	84
ox liver	0.23	3.1	13.4	0.83	110
average in liver	0.27	3.1	12.6	0.55	65
dried yeast (bakers')	2.33	4.0	36	2.0	trace only
yeast (brewers')	15.6				

Recommended daily intake in Britain for an adult man

1.4	1.6	18	2	3

What spoils a good story, if it has not just been spoiled, is that the same shelves that display these 'balanced' vitamin tablets also carry bottles of each of the separate B vitamins, so allowing you to upset the ratio even more.

In fact, balance is of no importance – which is just as well if you like bacon or liver. The body takes what it needs from our food and any excess of water-soluble vitamins – all the B vitamins are water-soluble – is washed out of the body.

BALANCED VITAMIN C

Vitamin C is ascorbic acid. It is claimed by health food advertisers that this will 'acidify the body' so you must buy their balanced vitamin C, ascorbic acid mixed with its sodium salt. There is no need for any such thing.

VITAMIN E

One manufacturer lists no less than twelve preparations of vitamin E in a single advertisement: 'natural' tablets of three strengths, 'natural' capsules in two strengths, fortified wheat germ capsules, a powder, a mixture with minerals (which in itself is very unnatural), chewable tablets and a mixture with polyunsaturated fatty acids. Which is balanced and which is best depends on the lady behind the counter.

Another claim for balanced vitamins accompanies a mixture said to be a supplement that 'ideally balances and enhances vitamin E'. It consists of calcium, vitamin C and vitamin B1. Not only do these substances have no connection whatsoever with vitamin E, but they have no connection with one another, so there can be no such thing as a balance of them.

CAN TOO MUCH BE HARMFUL?

It is difficult to believe that something essential to life, such as a vitamin, can be harmful when taken in excess, but an excess of virtually anything can be dangerous.

We need about 1 g of sodium (or approximately 2 g of sodium chloride, salt) daily. In this part of the world we take

153

on average 12 g of salt and some people take a great deal more. This is roughly one tenth of a fatal dose – 100 g of salt taken in a single dose is lethal. Obviously the body can get rid of the extra salt if it is taken over a full day but not if it is taken all at once.

Selenium is a highly toxic mineral, even small amounts can prove fatal, yet in extremely small amounts it is essential for life because it is part of some of our vital enzyme systems.

Perhaps the most dramatic example is that of water. Fluid of any kind is vital, but 3 litres of water, if drunk all at once, will kill you. In the same way, certain quantities of vitamins are essential, but larger amounts can be dangerous, and excessive amounts are lethal.

Among the most toxic of vitamins is D which normally helps the body to absorb calcium from food into the bloodstream and deposit it in the bones. When there is too much vitamin D, calcium is deposited in the soft tissues of the body resulting in damage and eventually death. Vitamin D is so toxic that it can be used as rat poison.

Vitamin A can also be harmful and it is even possible to get an excess from food, for instance such unusual items as polar bear or halibut liver. It has been known for some hundreds of years that polar bear liver is harmful – polar explorers were always warned by old hands. Early explorers developed drowsiness, headaches and peeling of the skin. No one knew why it was harmful until 1943 when scientists at Cambridge fed it to rats and traced the cause to very large quantities of vitamin A which the polar bear accumulates in its liver throughout its lifetime.

Polar bear liver may sound a rather exotic food, unlikely to be found on supermarket shelves, but damage from a more ordinary food was reported in 1970. Eleven fishermen caught a very big halibut, grilled the liver over a campfire and ate amounts varying from 30 g (1 oz) to 350 g (¾ lb). They suffered acute poisoning just five hours later, with peeling of the skin next day. The reason was that halibut liver – as the advertisement for halibut liver oil correctly states – is so rich in vitamin A that they had consumed doses between 1000 and 15,000 times that recommended as the amount needed daily.

In 1974 a man in Croydon, England, died from vitamin A poisoning – he had taken enormous doses in the hope of doing himself some good.

A letter in the *Lancet (3 March 1984)* pointed out the dangers of 'some of the "health" products (which) contain as much as 25,000 international units of vitamin A per tablet. The main danger is not immediate harm – very few cases of death from excessive doses of vitamin A have been reported – but from the fact that vitamin A in doses of the size sold in "health" food shops can damage the baby in the womb (teratogenic effect). These health foods are not licensed under the Medicines Act of 1968 but are sold as foods and so outside the control of the health authorities. Sooner or later the law will be amended but meanwhile this is evidence of the irresponsibility of people who purport to be selling "health" foods.'

Smaller doses can also have ill effects, especially if taken regularly over a period of time. The UK Medicines Act of 1968 limits the amounts of certain vitamins in tablets – not more than 2500 international units (750 micrograms) of vitamin A, 250 units (6 micrograms) of vitamin D, 25 micrograms of folic acid and 5 micrograms of vitamin B12. Larger doses, of course, may be used in medical treatment.

In his submission to the U.S. Sub-committee on Health, Linus Pauling stated that in his opinion, the toxicity of vitamins A and D has been over-emphasized. Yet nearly 600 cases of vitamin A poisoning have been reported in the scientific literature.

Even the Health Food Manufacturers' Association, which had long advocated extra vitamins, has now suggested limiting the amount of vitamin A in capsules to that recommended as the daily intake (2500 international units or 750 micrograms).

VITAMIN E

Contrary to the advice offered in so many health food shop leaflets, large doses of vitamin E can be harmful. A letter from a hospital published in the *British Medical Journal* in May 1978 reported a sudden and fatal rise in body temperature (known as malignant hyperthermia) after anaesthetic during an operation. This was thought to be due to overdosage with vitamin E. Although the exact amount the patient had been taking was not known, his blood levels were unusually high and it was thought that he had been taking about 200 mg twice daily – the amounts often recommended in 'health' magazines.

Vitamin E can interfere with vitamin K and it was shown as long ago as 1945 that large doses given to pregnant rats caused haemorrhage due to vitamin K shortage. In 1974 a man taking 1200 international units of vitamin E a day showed reduced blood coagulation until he stopped taking it. A report from Sweden showed prolonged blood clotting time in patients taking vitamin E.

EXPENSIVE URINE
It has been said that Americans have the most expensive urine in the world. This is because they take so many extra vitamin supplements that water-soluble vitamins (the Bs and C) are washed out of the body down the drains. Since water-soluble vitamins, unlike A, D, E and K, are not stored in the body to any great extent but are excreted it was thought that large doses must be harmless. This is not so. Toxic effects have been reported from excessive intakes of vitamin B1, niacin, B6, folic acid and vitamin C.

VITAMIN B6
The New England Journal of Medicine recently drew attention to seven cases (five women and two men) where severe nerve damage (peripheral neuropathy) developed after high doses of vitamin B6 were taken daily for up to forty months. The patients suffered from unsteadiness on the feet, numbness of the feet and clumsiness of the hands as the nerves were damaged. They improved after stopping the high doses, but even after six months still showed some diminished sensory perception. Four of the patients had taken the vitamin supplement of their own accord – so pointing out the dangers of the propaganda coming from high dose advocates. One

person had actually been advised by an orthomolecular psychiatrist.

Vitamin B6 is offered for sale as a 'pure powder' in 100 g bottles, making it almost impossible to take the small dose needed and highly probable that a dangerous overdose will occur.

FOLIC ACID

A shortage of vitamin B12, almost always due to poor absorption rather than a dietary deficiency, causes pernicious anaemia. This is much more serious than ordinary iron-deficiency anaemia because it leads to deterioration of the nervous system, a process that is often not reversible even if the vitamin is given by injection. The earliest signs are revealed by examining the blood before the nerves are damaged, but if large doses of folic acid are taken then the blood picture looks normal for a time, thus masking the disease. The damage to the nervous system therefore continues until it may be too late to treat.

For this reason, the U.S. Food and Drug Administration does not permit over the counter sales of folic acid in doses larger than 0.4 mg. Compare this with the Australian product, Nature's Way Health Foods, with 0.1 mg in a single tablet; Cantassium at 0.4 mg per tablet (Larkhall Laboratories, 1983 price list); 1.0 mg tablets offered at a reduced price if you buy four bottles; Cantassium 0.1 mg tablets in packs of 100; Sturdee Ger-e-time (an American brand recommending 6 tablets daily to make a total of 0.7 mg), presumably now banned; Nutro-hair (U.S.) 0.4 mg per tablet, recommending one with each meal so reaching a possible dose of 1.2–1.6 mg daily.

Doses of vitamin B1 as small as five times the recommended amount have been found to cause headaches, irritability, insomnia, rapid pulse and weakness.

MEGAVITAMIN THERAPY

Megavitamin therapy is based on the incorrect theory that

very large doses of vitamins confer special benefits on the consumer. It certainly seems to be an attractive theory – if a small dose of just a few milligrams can make the difference between life and death, then surely a large dose must confer even more benefit. But as with the spark plug analogy used earlier, there is nothing to be gained by exceeding the necessary limits.

The present vogue for megavitamin therapy stemmed from two sources. The first was the treatment of exceptionally rare diseases that some people are born with, known as inborn errors of metabolism. In such cases one of the enzymes does not properly cooperate with the vitamin it needs as its partner. A massive dose of the vitamin in question – B6 – was found to be the remedy. This illness is so rare that a doctor can pursue his entire career without meeting a case.

The second source was a novelist who 'felt' better and was convinced that he had fewer colds because he took large doses of vitamin C. Hearing this, Dr. Linus Pauling theorized that the amount of vitamin C needed by human beings should be based proportionately on the amount that a mouse makes for itself (animals can make their own vitamin C). Since a mouse weighs 20 g, multiplying this to reach the weight of an average man brought Dr. Pauling to the figure of 19 g as the requisite daily dose. Using the amount a goat makes for itself, he recommended that man should eat 13 g daily. The human body contains only 2–3 g of vitamin C altogether, which means that the theory is impractical and incorrect (*Evidence to the United States Senate Subcommittee on Health Vol. 1 No. 2*).

Another name for megavitamin therapy is orthomolecular medicine which means the right vitamins in the right quantity. Unfortunately the quantities are so far from being right that they are harmful. According to the theory each person needs a different dose of vitamins (this is probably quite true) but when daily doses up to 100 times the average are recommended, and the amount is greater than the total amount in the entire human body then the logic gets out of hand.

Large doses of vitamins are recommended for everything: vitamin C for backache, vitamin E for burns, hair shampoo and a number of other things, vitamin C to counteract the ill-effects (or some of the ill-effects) of smoking and vitamin B1 for tiredness.

Large doses of almost any vitamin, however, can be harmful, and the size of the doses recommended in ortho-molecular medicine are massive.

When nicotinic acid was first investigated back in 1938, scientists found that doses of 2 g a day caused dogs to develop convulsions in as short a time as twelve days. Although administration stopped after thirteen days, the dogs died on the nineteenth day. With a smaller dose of ½ g a day, the dogs excreted a trace of glucose and protein in their urine.

A wide variety of effects on the liver and heart as well as high blood levels of uric acid have been reported in people taking 3 g a day although one person developed jaundice with only 750 mg a day. Such doses are vastly in excess of the recommended intake of 20 mg daily but the megadose protagonists suggest 2–6 g daily for a variety of disorders (*Physicians' Handbook of Orthomolecular Medicine*).

Excessive intake of vitamin C has been associated with kidney stone, can affect the red blood cells and can impair the bacteria-killing function of the white blood cells. Such effects have been noted with doses of just 2 g a day – well within the amounts recommended by the megadose enthusiasts, but forty times as much as is recommended for vitamin function.

What may be of greater harm, because it is not so easily recognized, is the effect of large doses of vitamin C in damaging the ability of the body to rid itself of the harmful substances present in our foods (natural as well as added) and in the environment.

WITHDRAWAL SYMPTOMS

One of the problems created by vitamin overdose is that the body develops a mechanism to rid itself to some extent of the surplus. If you then stop taking large doses and return to normal, sensible amounts, the body continues to destroy and

159

eliminate the particular vitamin for some time. Real problems of deficiency can then result, and in the case of vitamin C, rebound scurvy can occur.

A report from Germany in 1958 stated that during the siege of Leningrad in World War II, people who had been receiving extra doses of vitamin C before the siege suffered a higher degree of scurvy than those who had not. A group of infants in Canada receiving adequate doses suffered from scurvy because their mothers had taken large doses during pregnancy and the babies had been conditioned to destroy it. Several other cases were listed in *Nutrition Reviews (November 1971)*; the authors called it 'dependence' on large doses. The effect was later demonstrated on guinea pigs in the laboratory.

Similar effects have been reported from vitamin B6. There are at least three medical reports of babies who had seizures because their mothers took doses of 5–300 mg daily during pregnancy. The seizures were due to a vitamin deficiency; the infants recovered when treated with B6.

Yet health food shops repeatedly claim that these 'natural' vitamins can confer enormous benefits, that they must be taken regularly and that they are, because they are called natural, completely harmless.

In a review of the toxic effects of water-soluble vitamins *(Nutrition Reviews, February 1984)*, sixteen disorders are listed which are aggravated by megadoses of water-soluble vitamins, including asthma, diabetes, liver disease, megaloblastic anaemia, cardiac diseases and disorders of the central nervous system.

LEGAL ACTION

A note headed 'Pregnancy risks leads to greater control on vitamin A' *(Pharmaceutical Journal, 3 December 1983)* referred to the fears of damaging effects on babies in the womb if their mothers took too much vitamin A. Although this particular effect has not been seen in women, it has been found in animals. Following advice from the Committee on Safety in

Medicines, the Health Minister decided to restrict high dose vitamin A products to doctors' prescriptions. Products on general sale should not contain more than 7500 international units, 2.25 mg, in a daily dose. The note states: 'The tighter control will apply only to products licensed under the Medicines Act and will not affect any vitamin A preparations sold as unlicensed products in outlets such as health food shops.'

DANGERS OF HEALTH FOODS

In an overview of food risks and hazards presented in 1982 to a symposium of the Association of Food and Drug Officials, Dr. Virgil Wodicka, formerly Director of the Bureau of Foods and the Food and Drug Administration in the United States made the telling point that we do not know the consequences of moderate overdoses for a lifetime for most of the essential nutrients. The opportunity for this kind of study has only occurred recently, since the synthesis of pure vitamins and, one might add, since the chemical extraction of concentrated forms of vitamins from natural foods.

WHAT IS A VITAMIN?

The term vitamin is applied scientifically to any substance found to be a dietary essential to living organisms, bacteria and insects included. It may not be essential to human beings and it is often difficult to find out whether it is or not.

Vitamin E, for example, was discovered in 1923 when rats given a purified diet with the addition of all the known vitamin concentrates were unable to reproduce. Their sterility was cured by giving them certain vegetable oils. When the vitamin was isolated in a pure form in 1936 it was called tocopherol from the Greek for 'child-bearing'. It does not have any effect on human child-bearing.

Because many experimental and farm animals needed this

substance it was classified a vitamin. But since there were no cases of deficiency among human beings, was it in fact a vitamin for man? The first evidence that it was essential did not come to light until 1951 because of failure to absorb the vitamin after surgery of the intestine. Several months after their operations, patients showed the signs of deficiency that had been seen in animals – low blood levels of vitamin E, red blood cells that could be broken down rather easily and brown pigment deposited in the walls of the intestine. So it is essential and must be classified as a vitamin for man although no one has ever been known to suffer any disease caused by a dietary shortage.

Promoters of vitamin E have described it as the granddaddy of vitamins and the 'atomic bomb of medicine'. It is popularly, and incorrectly, thought of as the fertility vitamin, but this is only true for rats and mice. Different animals show different effects when suffering a deficiency: rabbits and guinea pigs develop muscular dystrophy; pigs suffer liver damage; chickens show signs of brain damage. Only in rats and mice does a deficiency affect reproduction. The only human beings needing supplements are premature babies who have a particular kind of anaemia which responds to vitamin E. But the tales of its effect on fertility and virility persist, even amongst medical students who recite a poem which includes the line 'we'll blast the hopes of Marie Stopes by taking it with our tea'.

Dr. Rynearson stated in *Nutrition Reviews (July 1974, Vol. 32)* that the list of conditions for which vitamin E has been recommended is limited only by one's imagination – high blood pressure, Buerger's disease, gangrene, nephritis, acute rheumatic fever, vascular complications of diabetes, angina pectoris, atherosclerosis, coronary thrombosis, varicose veins, aid to healing wounds and burns and, if taken when young, to prevent sterility, senility and stroke. All of this is nonsense.

Nor is it harmless because in large amounts, of the size recommended by megadose enthusiasts, it has caused headaches, nausea and blurred vision. There is one possible, albeit unproven, virtue which may indicate that doses of a few milligrams daily might possibly be beneficial and cannot do any harm. Vitamin E acts in fats as a preservative or antioxidant and is added to processed foods as such. One of the numerous theories of aging is that the fat in the cell walls of the body tissues oxidize so it is possible that vitamin E might help. On the other hand it might not, or we might already receive enough in our daily diet to make any extra superfluous, but in small amounts it can do no harm and hope springs eternal.

Vitamin E preparations from health food shops range from 200 international units (200 mg) up to 1200 international units. The smaller amount is five times the recommended daily intake according to U.S. authorities – UK authorities do not make any recommendations for this vitamin. The larger amount is thirty times the recommended daily amount.

Claims for the benefits of vitamin E to sufferers of atherosclerosis have been largely disproved. An experiment was conducted amongst eighteen volunteers, each of whom took 600 international units daily for 28 days. There was no effect at the end of that time on their blood cholesterol or their blood triglycerides (*Proceedings of the Nutrition Society, July 1982*). At the same time, there is evidence that even people on poor diets get enough vitamin E. An investigation among the poorest groups of migrant workers in Boia-Frias, Brazil, showed that both the infants and the adults had the same level in their blood as did well-fed infants and adults in the United States and Canada (*American Journal of Clinical Nutrition, December 1980, pp. 2669–2673*).

The health food approach is admirably summed up in *Health Now (January 1979, Issue No. 5)* which says 'if you are interested in natural vitamin supplements you will soon read that vitamin E is one of the most valuable of nutrients – that is unless you happen to speak to a scientist and then you will be told that vitamin E has no known nutritional value to humans.' This is not quite true – scientists will in fact tell you that vitamin E, being a vitamin, is a dietary essential. No one could say that it has no known nutritional value, but it can be said that apart from premature babies, extra vitamin E does not have any value. Holland and Barrett (*Natural Choice No. 14*) correctly and honestly stated that because of the lack of full scientific evidence, neither they nor advertisers could claim good effects for this practice (of people taking large doses of vitamin E every day). They did, however, suggest that the potential customer read a book on vitamin E which makes the usual extravagant claims.

VITAMIN F

No one outside the health food business uses the name vitamin F any longer. In 1929 it was found that rats failed to grow on a purified diet containing all the known vitamins until a vegetable oil was added. The curative substance was found to be a pair of fatty acids – linoleic and linolenic – which were therefore classed as a vitamin and collectively called F. This term was soon dropped and the two ingredients simply became known as the essential fatty acids. Linolenic acid is essential for human beings although any dietary shortage is very unusual. There is a certain type of eczema in babies that responds to it and it has to be included in mixtures given to patients intravenously. Except for these few babies, dietary shortages do not occur because the amount needed is only 2–4 grams a day and this seems to be present in all diets even in poor communities.

Statements that 'many people are deficient in vitamin F' (Michael Wheatley in *A Way of Living as a Means of Survival*) are quite untrue.

There is another, quite different aspect of these fatty acids concerned in heart disease. Saturated fats increase the levels of cholesterol in the blood and are thus associated with heart disease. Linolenic acid and several other related fatty acids (which are not, however, dietary essentials) can counteract the effect of saturated fats to some extent and reduce blood cholesterol levels. These are collectively known as the polyunsaturated fatty acids, a term frequently used on the labels of special margarines made from sunflower and corn oils among others. For this purpose the amount of poly-unsaturated fatty acids needs to be about one quarter to one half of the total fat intake.

PABA

PABA, para-amino benzoic acid, has been shown to be essential to some bacteria but no deficiency has ever been reported in either human beings or animals. It is used as a sun-screen to prevent sunburn but since it can cause dermatitis has been banned in some countries. Claims for its virtues are completely without foundation.

PANTOTHENIC ACID

Pantothenic acid has been shown to be essential in the diet of rats, chickens and dogs but no deficiency has ever been found in human beings. It is widely distributed in foods – vegetables, liver, kidney and yeast – and is present in all living cells as an essential part of the cell mechanism.

Since it has never been found to be in short supply, there is no validity to claims made for it as a dietary supplement. In fact, tablets of pantothenic acid are an excellent example of wasted money, since 70 per cent is excreted in the urine and the remainder passes through the intestine to be excreted in the faeces making a 100 per cent dead loss. But it is sold with the misleading claim that it is easily destroyed in cooking and the tablets 'merely replace a vital substance so wantonly destroyed in cooking and food processing'.

NON-EXISTENT VITAMINS

Some vitamins exist only in the imagination of health food promoters. Occasionally laboratory animals grow unusually well on certain diets, giving rise to hopes that a new growth factor has been discovered but then the experiment cannot be repeated and the hopes are dashed. We do not know all the factors that control growth and sometimes get unusual results when dealing with living organisms. Unconfirmed reports of growth factors for chickens, mice or insects can be found in scientific literature which later proved groundless. Most research workers confirm their findings before publishing their reports but there are a few articles to be found proclaiming new vitamins. It is these which are sometimes cited by health food promoters. The B vitamins are a perfect

165

example of these misconceptions. B3 was the number assigned, at one stage, to pantothenic acid and sometimes wrongly appled to niacin. B4 was given to a mixture that later turned out to be three amino acids. B5 is somewhat uncertain since it was the name used for a growth factor that turned out to be vitamin B6 or, according to some research workers, niacin. Vitamins B7, B8 and B9 have never been used, leaving scope for a newcomer.

The three currently being exploited by health food shops are the nonexistent B13, B15 and B17. For reasons known only to themselves, the people who christened a well-known chemical B17 failed to notice that B16 had never been used. I myself have questioned this in a short article entitled *Whatever happened to B16?* which will presumably be quoted when a health food supplement is marketed under this title. There have also been references in scientific journals to vitamin G, once used for B2; L1 and L2 which were never confirmed; vitamin M, now known to be one of the forms of folic acid; vitamin T which turned out to be a mixture of known chemicals; Factor I and Factor T which were used for B6; Factor U which is a derivative of an amino acid; Factor W which is an old name for biotin or vitamin H, and Factor X which was commonly used when scientists could not identify it but mostly used in the early days for B12.

These names reflect not only unexplained and inexplicable laboratory results, but also the inevitable confusion that arose when hundreds of laboratories all over the world were investigating foods that supported growth. Different names were bound to be assigned to substances which were eventually discovered to be the same thing. So health food promoters can almost always 'prove' that they are selling a factor or vitamin with 'evidence' culled from scientific literature. The truth is that this evidence is not always acceptable as it was not always confirmed and in many instances was later shown to be incorrect.

VITAMIN B13

Orotic acid is formed in the cells of the body from one of the amino acids (aspartic acid) and is then changed into the various pyrimidines which are present in the nuclei of cells in all parts of the body. It is not needed in the diet (although there is some in milk), it does no good to take any and a small amount is always excreted in the urine.

Orotic acid does appear to be essential for certain bacteria which cannot grow without it, so it is not incorrect to call it a vitamin, even though it is not a vitamin for any animal, including man.

Health food purveyors, however, call orotic acid 'a natural vitamin-mineral bridge' which is pure invention. Furthermore they claim that it plays an important part in the body's utilization of minerals, a statement which is simply not true. There has been a trend among health food manufacturers – in keeping with their unfounded claim that it is a vitamin-mineral bridge – to make iron, magnesium and other metal salts of orotic acid and claim that they are particularly valuable to health. They are not.

VITAMIN B14
This is a substance of no importance found in human urine and thought by its finder to be a growth factor and hence a vitamin but not even health food shops sell it.

VITAMIN B15
B15 is not a vitamin at all, but a chemical called pangamic acid first discovered in 1951 in apricot kernels and rice bran. The name comes from the Greek 'pan' for universal and 'gamic' for seeds because it was found in so many seeds. It was also found later in brewer's yeast, liver and many cereals. So even if it does do good, it is found in so many foods that we already get enough in our ordinary diet. No specific disease is associated with either its presence or its absence. It is not a dietary essential, hence it is not a vitamin. It has been injected into mice and does not seem to be very harmful, but no one as yet has tested it for safety.

It has no known function in human beings but this has not prevented manufacturers from claiming special virtues for it.

At one time in Australia health food shops run by the very people who object to chemicals in food were plastered with signs claiming all the wonders of the world for this particular chemical.

VITAMIN B17 (see Laetrile, page 81)
Apart from the incorrect claim that it cures cancer, and the deaths reported from the cyanide in laetrile, B17 is advertised as the magical food eaten by people of the Hunza Valley 'who live to an extremely ripe old age'. It is claimed to be the major dietary difference between them and modern Western man – presumably they, too, have hamburgers, fish and chips and take-away chicken! Further, the advertisements claim that 'the fact that it is virtually absent from civilized diets has been claimed to be an important factor in the health problems associated with modern living' (*advertisement in Cantassium Health Standard*).

The manufacturers cover themselves legally by stating about both 'vitamins' B15 and B17 'we cannot legally make any health claims for the substances' – just after making those quoted above. The sale of B17 over the counter has been forbidden since early 1984 because it is toxic.

VITAMIN TABLETS – TO TAKE OR NOT TO TAKE

Nutritionists are frequently asked whether it is worthwhile taking vitamin tablets. Some reply that they are unnecessary because a good diet will provide all that we need. This is quite true, but leads to the next question – how do we know if we're following a good diet?

If you are not sure that you are following a good diet, vitamin tablets can be taken as insurance. The Advertising Standards Association in Great Britain, and other bodies concerned with advertising, have laid down a Code of Practice whereby claims for the benefits of vitamin tablets are restricted to certain vulnerable groups of the population.

Pregnant women who need to be sure that the infant in the womb is fully supplied with all the necessary nutrients, lactating mothers who are supplying food to both themselves and their babies, and young children whose rapid growth rate might be restricted if their diet was in any way deficient are included in these groups. In addition, children whose faddy eating habits could lead to relatively poor diets might find extra vitamin tablets beneficial.

Adolescents frequently eat snacks at odd times instead of meals, or follow slimming or cult diets. At that time of life they have an enhanced need for nutrients and they therefore comprise another group that is considered vulnerable. Finally, some elderly people live on a restricted diet, may not absorb some vitamins as well as healthy young adults do or even have greater requirements. After almost any illness the body stores of vitamins must be rebuilt so here again supplements are particularly valuable and even, in some cases, necessary.

As far as the average adult is concerned, though, vitamin supplements should be looked on as an insurance policy, just to be sure that they are getting enough. With the wide range of food available in industrialized countries, not even those living on snack foods and making a poor choice of diet could be so short of any vitamin that real signs of deficiency would appear. Cases of beri-beri (vitamin B1 deficiency), pellagra (niacin deficiency), or scurvy (C deficiency) just do not arise in Western countries. The only vitamin problem seen regularly among some sections of the population is rickets, shortage of vitamin D.

What will happen then to people who are only slightly short of a vitamin? Nothing very obvious – they may catch influenza more easily or recover more slowly, or their tissues might be less resistant to stress – but these problems might just as easily be due to other causes. It is virtually impossible to prove that they are due to a vitamin shortage.

Any shortfall in general health standards due to a shortfall in vitamin intake would be too small to measure. Likewise any improvement resulting from taking vitamin tablets, apart from the placebo effect of faith, would be too small to measure.

So using tablets as a form of insurance is still fairly uncertain. Small amounts will not do any harm and they might possibly do some good. But they do not even need to be taken daily. However poor our diet, we are eating something and getting some vitamins which means that one tablet taken on alternate days would be sufficient.

This is not the philosophy of the health food supplement lobby. They not only advocate large doses and advertise powerful tablets, but actually list the disorders you may be suffering from due to a shortage of vitamins. Those listed are actually the signs of acute deficiencies, as seen in some developing countries, but never seen in the West. For example, beri-beri is never seen in this part of the world except amongst chronic alcoholics who eat very few of the foods containing B1. One of the signs of this disease is damage to the nerves, called nervous irritability in text books. Health food advertisements use this to claim that B vitamins give relief from nervous irritability and over-excitement (whatever that means), and also 'dispel lethargy', another symptom of beri-beri.

VITAMINS

Letter	Name	Function in body	Where to find it
A	retinol; carotene	growth; maintains moist mucous tissues in healthy condition; night vision	liver, milk fat, margarine, leafy green vegetables, yellow and orange fruits and vegetables
B1	thiamin	liberation of energy from foods	cereals, (especially whole grain) meat; liver; peanuts; yeast
B2	riboflavin	liberation of energy from foods	liver; milk; meats; cheese
—	niacin	liberation of energy from foods	same as B1
C	ascorbic acid	maintenance of cementing substance between cells	fruits and vegetables
D	cholecalciferol	absorption of calcium from the diet; deposition of calcium on bones	margarine, eggs, fatty fish – and sunshine
E	tocopherol	fat preservative	cereals, wheat germ, some fruits and vegetables, fish, meat, eggs
B6	pyridoxine	metabolism of proteins	fish, meats
B12	cobalamin	blood formation	meats, especially liver; beer
—	pantothenic acid	metabolism of food	fish, some fruits
—	folic acid	blood formation	fruits and vegetables, liver
H	biotin	metabolism of food	fruits and vegetables

7

DIETS
AND SLIMMING

Being 'on a diet' means slimming to most people. In fact, we are always 'on a diet' because whatever we are eating is our diet. Apart from slimming, people change their eating habits, or 'go on a diet', for a variety of reasons. Some of us become vegetarians for economic or religious reasons. There are some religious practices in which the diet is only partly restricted, e.g. pork, beef, tea, coffee or alcohol are avoided. Some traditional practices also encourage various foods – chicken is highly prized in Malaysia, honey in health food magazines. There are also a number of food 'cults', including fashion. If a film star, sports hero or well-publicized journalist starts a trend for peanuts, baked beans or brown rice, followers always appear. Most cults are harmless, but one which has caused countless problems is the so-called Zen Macrobiotic Diet.

ZEN MACROBIOTIC DIET

Several people following this diet have died. Its adherents pass through ten stages of increasing dietary restriction until they are eating only cereals. Severe nutritional deficiencies may result (*British Medical Journal, April 1978; American Academy Pediatric Clinics of North America 1977, Vol. 24, p. 189*). *Which? (June 1978)* described the macrobiotic diet as 'very dangerous' and added the caution 'the philosophy (of Eastern mysticism) may attract you; beware of the diets.'

The diet progresses from one that is nutritionally adequate, although based on way-out ideas, to one that is so restricted that malnutrition is not only likely, but has occurred and resulted in some deaths.

Stage three, the starting point, includes 10 per cent of food from cereal, 30 per cent from vegetables, 10 per cent soup, 30 per cent animal products, 15 per cent fruit and salad, 5 per cent desserts. The final and highest level, diet seven, consists entirely of cereals. This not only achieves the desired state of mental and physical well-being, they say, but cures cancer! 'No macrobiotic person can be a victim of illness' is the claim made for the diet. While some of us might consider such farfetched and outlandish claims unbelievable, so many American adolescents followed the diet – partly as a revolt against authority and partly because of our eternal hopes for everlasting peace, life and happiness – that the American Medical Association issued several warnings to the public. Cases of scurvy, anaemia, low blood protein, low blood calcium and loss of kidney function through restriction of fluid intake have all been reported.

In 1973 (*Lancet, 9 June*) a group of American doctors reported on a Zen macrobiotic baby food called Kokoh consisting of sweet brown rice, aduki beans, soya beans, oats, sesame seeds and wheat. The mixture sounds adequate but the amounts allowed to the babies were far too small. Two infants arrived in hospital severely malnourished. One, aged 7 months, weighed only 11 lb; the other, aged 14 months, weighed 13 lb. Both were extremely short in length. Their energy intake was only 40 per cent of what it should have been so the babies were burning up their own protein tissues to provide energy. Advice on feeding the babies on this macrobiotic system was given in Macroguide No. 10 which advises diluting milk to such levels that infants could not get enough food into their small stomachs.

Michio Kushi in *The Book of Macrobiotics – the Universal Way to Health and Happiness* explains that everything, not just food, is either yin or yang. Warmth, humidity and soft textures are yin while cold, dry and hard are yang. Strangely, cool body temperatures are yin and warm temperatures are yang. Tall is yin, short is yang; cooking is yin but slower cooking is yang; large spaces such as continents where there are tales of giants are yin, islands which are small and which have tales about midgets and leprechauns are yang.

The book goes on at length, and in great detail. Your date of birth determines whether you are yin or yang. A vast list of diseases, disorders and emotions are classified and the reader is told that certain foods must be eaten to get particular effects. Carp, clams, watermelon, potatoes, plums, quail, sugar, honey, garlic and ice water are yin. Horsemeat, buckwheat, duck and hen eggs, pork and caviar are yang.

Even vitamins are subdivided. B1, B2, niacin, folic acid, C and B12 are yin while A, D, E, K and B6 are yang. The basis of this breakdown is not only oriental mysticism, but a scientific mystery. Since 'all our problems are caused by the incorrect mixtures of yin and yang in our food and environment', so they are cured by the appropriate mixtures of yin and yang. Likewise health, joy and happiness are ensured by the correct balance.

Balfour and Allen (*The A to Z of Health Food Terms*) describe macrobiotics as the art of choosing food that will make your life more adventurous, amusing, happy and healthy. They say that grains used within the principles of macrobiotics can actually be weight-reducing factors – a statement which is completely untrue. Inactivity, day-dreaming, hair loss and poor circulation are, they say, signs of an extremely yin condition, caused by taking too much sugar, fruit, dairy produce and drugs. Anger, hostility and excessive masculinity are a result of eating too much meat. And salt is very yang. Just to make things even more difficult, the balance of yin and yang foods has to be changed to suit the climate.

Followers of this cult will be disappointed to learn that baldness cannot be cured even with a macrobiotic diet. Baldness around the peripheral regions of the head is yin, central baldness is yang and complete baldness is a combination of the two, so there is no balance of food which will put hair back on.

RASTAFARIANS

The Rastafarian diet is another cult which is generally harmless, but for one thing. *The British Medical Journal (December 1982)* reported the case of ten Rastafarian men, aged 18–40, who had lived exclusively on vegetarian diets for periods varying from two to twenty years. The men came to Kingston Hospital, Jamaica with a number of symptoms, including neurological ones, due to a deficiency of vitamin B12. All but one responded to treatment with B12. The man who was the exception died eleven days after being admitted to the hospital.

SLIMMING

Slimming diets dwarf everything else in the food field. Slimming involves not just diets, but so-called slimming aids – books, recipes, pills, drugs, chemicals, exercise machinery, clothing and special foods.

There is full agreement among all health authorities that obesity is a killer. Overweight people have greatly increased chances of heart attack, diabetes, diseases of the joints and a vast number of other disorders. Obesity can lead to early death. Strangely enough – such is human nature – these horrors are frequently not as important to fat people as the fact that they cannot wear fashionable clothes, that their children are often ashamed of them, and that they cannot participate in many of the ordinary activities going on around them. So deeply do they feel these problems that at any given moment about a fifth of the population of the entire industrialized world is 'on a diet', thinking of going on a diet, going to a health farm or buying a 'slimming aid'.

Hence the enormous appeal of slimming cures. In fact there are no cures. It is now illegal in Great Britain to make claims for any slimming aid of any kind except as part of a calorie-controlled diet. People get fat because they have been consuming more calories than they are using. We can lose weight only if we reverse the process, that is, eat less calories than we use.

The commonly used term 'diet' implies that you are changing your eating pattern for the period of time needed to lose weight. But what happens then? Most of us return to our old habits and regain the fat lost 'on the diet'. The only long-term solution is to learn new eating habits and keep them for life.

All of this is very difficult, so any slimming aid advertised, whether surgery of the intestine, stapling the stomach to make it smaller, pills or special food, is anxiously sought at any price by vast numbers of hopeful – and by this time usually hopeless – people.

DIETS AND DIETING

Those who live in hopes of a 'cure' for their weight problem cannot be blamed for clutching at straws. And there are certainly vast numbers of straws available – the *Consumer Guide* in the United States lists one hundred current diets. Of these, twenty-five are given zero on a four-star rating, which means 'they are not recommended', and are described as being unrealistic or dangerous to health. The extremely well sold Beverly Hills Diet and the Cambridge Formula Diet are both included in this group. There were also a few one-star diets, described as foolish but not dangerous and which might, in certain circumstances, be useful. Of the remainder, twenty-three are given two stars, meaning that they may be harmful to some people; twenty-five rate three stars, meaning that they are low in protein and fat but too different to the public taste to be palatable. Only twenty-seven out of one hundred listed earned four stars – meaning that they were nutritionally good, likely to be helpful and likely to be followed. The rating system, incidentally, includes the probability of people sticking to the diet.

So there is quite a choice, with one hundred diets plus supplements, bath dissolvers, fat solvents and pills all widely available.

HELPING THE WILL POWER

Very few people stay on a diet long enough to lose much

weight, so new ones appear regularly. Some are exactly the same as old ones, but with new names and different sales promotion. A recent American textbook on nutrition lists twelve low-carbohydrate diets, starting with the Banting Diet in 1870 and progressing through the Dupont Diet, Drinking Man's Diet, Air Force Diet, Airline Pilots' Diet (one wonders why these two should differ if indeed either the Air Force or airlines had anything to do with them), Astronauts' Diet (astronauts really need feeding rather than slimming), the Miracle Diet, Thinking Man's Diet (brain food?), Carbo-Cal Diet, Number 10, McCall's Snack Diet and the Wisconsin Diet. Any or all of them could work because they supply only 1000 Calories a day and we can all lose surplus fat on such a low amount – if we stick to the diet long enough. What few people realize is that it takes months or years to gain weight and it cannot, therefore, be lost in just a few days.

There are also several high protein diets – Does-It Diet, Lazy Lady Diet and Dr. Quick Inches Off. To add to the variety, if not the cure, there are high fat-high protein-low carbohydrate diets. If the diets don't suit you, you can try such alternatives as drugs, surgery and starvation. Or you could just pinch your ears when you feel hungry!

PILLS, BATHS AND MACHINES

As dieting is so difficult, couldn't we find a magic wand to remove the fat? Although the true answer would have to be 'no', there are many products which claim that they can do just that. There are pills that 'dissolve the fat away' and turn out to be no more than vitamin tablets; there are bath salts that also 'dissolve the fat away' and there are machines and clothing claimed to 'burn off' the fat under the skin. None of them works.

STARCH BLOCKERS

Some of the best-selling 'magic' pills in recent years were the starch blockers. The principle behind them was simple – if we could stop the body digesting starch then half of our food (since half of what we eat is starch) would pass straight through the body. This means that we could eat as much as we like and simply pass the excess down the drains.

Unfortunately the principle does not, and cannot, work. There are four good reasons. First, the body produces enough of the enzyme (amylase) to digest 9 kg of starch. Since we eat about 300 g daily, we have at least thirty times as much of this enzyme as we need. Second, the starch blocker is a protein substance that interferes with the starch-digesting enzyme (amylase). It works very well in a test-tube if you leave the enzyme and anti-enzyme mixed together for a while, but when the starch blocker is eaten it is digested in the stomach just like any other food protein.

To understand the third reason, try to imagine what would happen if it did stop the digestion of starch. The flatulence, or wind, which results from eating peas and beans is caused by the 2–3 g of indigestible sugar they contain. The sugar passes down the intestine until it reaches the part where bacteria live. The bacteria flourish and produce gas. If the 300 g of starch we eat daily was not digested (as the salesmen tell us), it would all be passed down to feed the bacteria, which would flourish and produce even more gas. So if the starch blockers worked, the would-be slimmer would probably burst!

Finally, we know from laboratory experiments with rats what would happen if starch blockers did work. Experiments were carried out on protein blockers rather than starch blockers because many raw beans contain trypsin inhibitors which block the enzyme (trypsin) that digests protein. When large amounts of beans are fed to a rat it quickly adapts and its pancreas produces more trypsin. After a few weeks on such a diet the rat's pancreas becomes enlarged. It is likely, therefore, that if the starch blocker worked on human beings, our pancreas would become enlarged. Any enlargement of an organ is potentially cancerous, so starch blockers are potentially carcinogenic.

Fortunately they do not work, but they did sound like a very good idea. Before starch blockers were withdrawn in June 1982, the consumption in the United States was ten million tablets a week (*Chemistry and Industry, 21 February 1983*).

Some of the hundreds of preparations sold were impure and toxic. When purified properly the substance is harmless and just adds four calories per gram to the ordinary diet.

After the American ban, stocks were immediately shipped to England. Several scientific papers have been published showing that starch blockers are useless, but health food shops have taken them up on a large scale. In *ASA Case Report 97 (May 1983)* the Advertising Standards Authority declared itself deeply concerned that, notwithstanding the advice on an advertisement contained in the Code of Practice, a company known as Goodscale Laboratories had submitted its advertisements for starch blockers. These had been accepted by several newspapers. The advertisers failed to respond to the Authority's enquiries and the Authority had to remind the media that the advertisers had failed to substantiate their claims. The claims were that 'starch blocker TM is an amazing discovery that lets you eat your favourite starch foods but keeps your body from absorbing all those fat-producing calories. One tablet can block up to 400 Calories from starch.' A 'free offer for the first 100 replies' was not available because supplies were exhausted, but the advertisement continued to say that free samples were on offer.

One of the advertisements for 'Newton's Traditional Remedies' claimed that taking one before a meal allowed you to enjoy potatoes, bread, chips, pasta etc. and so lose weight painlessly. The advertisers were unable to substantiate these claims *(ASA Case Report 94, Feb. 1983)*.

Another company, Starchblock, went so far as to submit evidence to defend their claim to the Advertising Standards Authority *(Case Report 94, Feb. 1983)* but this was rejected by the Authority's independent medical consultant because it did not substantiate the safety and efficiency of this system of weight reduction.

As recently as September 1983, long after being banned in the United States, the President of the Health Food Manufacturers Association in Great Britain still fought a delaying action by stating: 'I do not believe that we have heard the end of alpha-amylase starch blockers which may well have a place in helping diabetics' and 'we have seen many letters from members of the public who have found both (starch blockers and spirulina) to be effective' *(Chemistry and Industry, 5 Sept. 1983)*.

CLAIMS AND MORE CLAIMS

Low-calorie foods are regularly added to the shelves, along with slimming aids such as low-calorie meal replacers, slimming machines and countless slimming swindles. Although the latter are generally taken to court for infringing regulations, new ones appear so rapidly that the market is steadily increasing. They include simple vitamin tablets labelled with dishonest claims that they can help achieve a weight loss.

The Advertising Standards Authority wisely stated (Sept. 1982): 'the only practical way to lose weight is by changing either the way you eat or how much you eat.' 'Wonders will happen' it quotes from an advertiser, and continues 'but no miracle yet invented can make you lose weight safely. Exercise alone is not enough. Electrically charged pads may firm your muscles but neither will make you weigh less ... Wonders such as inches lost in 90 minutes or 5 cm off for the price of a phone call sadly do not happen and such claims bring no credit either to the advertiser or the publisher who accepts such spurious advertising claims.'

In line with these views, a complaint was upheld against an advertisement for a slimming machine that would cause the customer to lose up to six inches of fat in one hour *(ASA Case Report 92, Dec. 1982)*. A similar complaint was upheld against an advertisement for 'effortless slimming with Hawkins Home Slimming System. Simply lie down, flick on the computerized, space-age EBA-16 and your muscles will immediately begin the slimming process.' Still another advertisement which was rejected was for the Maximum Loss Capsule Diet Plan which stated 'you can lose 7 lb in three days, 16 lb in one week, 24 lb in two weeks ... Completely safe to take –contains no drugs or chemicals' *(ASA Case Report 98, June 1983)*. Advertisements which include statements such as 'I lost 16 lb in seven days' using a 'fantastic new diet capsule' are untrue, impossible and contrary to the regulations.

It is now illegal in Great Britain to make any claim for weight reduction unless the advertisement specifies 'as part of a calorie controlled diet'. No food is slimming – they are all fattening if you eat enough. There is no capsule that can remove fat. But the impossible part of the claim is the amount said to be lost. Even if you starved completely – in itself extremely dangerous – you would supply one week's need of 14,000–17,500 Calories (seven times the daily 2000–2500) from 4–5 lb of fat. So claims that 16 lb can be lost in seven days are untrue, and to claim that this can be achieved while eating normally is obviously impossible.

The list of outrageous claims is endless, though:

'Slim with Modatrop, one tablet in the morning and one at noon during meals will lead to prompt decrease in body weight, without adherence to a strict diet, well tolerated, and non-habit forming' *(ASA Report 94, Feb. 1983)*.

Trimite International (Beptrim) – 'lose 2 inches in one hour' *(ASA Report 95, March 1983)*;

'21st century slimming and beauty clinic – guaranteed weight loss and an inch lost – fast and easy. Our new Frigithalgo treatment along with spot reduction thermic cellutherm will help you to lose weight' *(ASA Report 95, March 1983)*.

MULTIPLE MAGIC
Five substances are frequently claimed to help slimming – spirulina, lecithin, kelp, vitamin B6 and modified cotton wool. All but the last are fully described elsewhere, but a few of the untrue claims made for them as slimming aids can be outlined here.

Spirulina, the plant alga, is claimed quite incorrectly to depress the appetite. According to an article in the free Australian handout *Healthy Life News*, it 'has proven to be a very successful weight reducing agent'. It is said to be so good that you lose weight even if you go on an eating binge and crave fattening sweets. Not true.

Lecithin is a type of fat that is made in the body from other parts of the diet. As discussed in Chapter 3, it is added to ice cream and chocolate and is naturally present in eggs. It is claimed to be a slimming aid because it breaks up fatty globules in the bloodstream. Not true.

Kelp is seaweed. Claims for its value as a slimming aid appear to be based on its content of iodine. The thyroid gland produces the hormone thyroxine which controls the rate of body metabolism and thyroxine does include iodine in its molecule, but iodine itself – whether from tablets, seaweed or food – has no effect.

Vitamin B6, it is said, 'seems' to assist the body to break down carbohydrates. In fact this vitamin is not concerned with the metabolism of carbohydrates but with proteins (amino acids) and it has no connection with speeding up any process that might lead to weight loss.

Cotton wool is cellulose and can be chemically treated to give methyl cellulose which swells in water. The idea behind taking modified cotton wool before a meal with a glass of water is that it will swell in the stomach and stop you eating as much as you would normally. Although this may sound an attractive idea, it does not work and there is certainly no effect with the amount sold in capsules and tablets. The right material, carboxymethyl cellulose, in a particular crystalline form, can absorb up to fifty times its weight of water, but the amount in a tablet or capsule is usually one quarter of one gram. Even if it did swell fifty times, that only makes twelve and one half grams, or about half of a fluid ounce. The stomach holds several pints and is very elastic, so half an ounce is not even noticeable.

In addition, some methyl cellulose tablets are fattening because they are made up with glucose at the rate of four Calories to every gram. This means that taking some 'slimming' tablets can result in taking extra calories.

Manufacturers try to sell these various slimming aids separately and in combination. An article in *Which?* *(September 1983)* starts: 'Lose that beauty-robbing fat ran the ad from Dietcare International.' For £16.45 customers received fourteen bottles of pills to be taken before meals containing

1 hungerstoppers (bulking agents that are supposed to swell up in the stomach and make you feel full before even starting to eat)
2 starch blockers
3 something called a fat-burner (lecithin)
4 a so-called appetite curber (spirulina)
5 a multi-vitamin pill
6 a so-called energizer (with ginseng)

Which? had already discussed starch blockers and bulking agents and politely told their readers not to waste their money. Spirulina and lecithin were equally dismissed as having no value for slimming. 'No evidence that spirulina curbs the appetite ... No evidence that lecithin helps to lose weight.'

A similar Cantassium product contains 125 mg lecithin, 60 mg cider vinegar (also alleged to be a slimming aid), 50 mg kelp and 5 mg vitamin B6 in each tablet of S-40 slimmers supplement. The product advertised in the Australian leaflet mentioned earlier adds yet another wonder of the modern world, alfalfa grass, usually reserved for feeding cattle. The ad does not explain why this should help anyone to slim and it is impossible to make a guess. This product is doubly useful however, because it helps people put on weight as well as take it off! It is claimed to be of value to people recovering from illness, or just plain run down, who cannot tolerate eating much.

CASHING IN ON FAMOUS NAMES

Some salesmen of questionable products have no compunction about using the names of scientists or organizations who have never had any connection with them. One such product, advertised widely in a number of countries, says that it is 'a London University Crash-burn wonder diet ... the fastest weight loss method known to medical science' (except for total starvation). It goes on to claim that it burns off fat four times faster than high-speed diets (surely this must be faster than total starvation) and eleven times faster than exercise (this claim would depend on the type of exercise and how long it was kept up – the statement is worse than meaningless).

Furthermore 'it melts down fat like hot water melts down ice'. Unfortunately nothing melts down fat in the body, it has to be used up as energy. A claim is also made that you can lose up to 1 lb in 8 hours which is, indeed, faster than total starvation.

Finally, it claims that a government official lost 10 lb in 72 hours, although why the experience of a government official should be regarded as useful advertising is open to question. Apart from its claim to have been invented by scientists of London University – which is not true – it also refers to scientists at the University of California – equally untrue. Claims of this kind are illegal in Great Britain, but while the legal machinery is set in motion the manufacturers are taking their profits. Once they are stopped they can market another product until that, in its turn, is stopped.

GRAPEFRUIT

Advertisements for the recently popular grapefruit diet claimed 'Lose 10 lb in 10 days without pills or drugs ... We have testimonials reporting on its success'. After the initial weight loss, it claimed that you could lose $1\frac{1}{2}$ lb every two days until you got down to your proper weight. This is not possible, particularly as you can continue to eat 'forbidden foods such as steaks, roast or fried chicken, gravies, mayonnaise, lobster swimming in butter, bacon fat, scrambled eggs and still lose weight'. The 'secret' of this diet is revealed when you send your money for the grapefruit diet plan.

The grapefruit diet led one manufacturer to market Dieter's grapefruit tablets. The Advertising Standards Authority found that the advertiser could not produce evidence of a medical and scientific nature to support the claim that grapefruit tablets were in any way effective in assisting users to stick to their diet (*Case Report 97, May 1983*).

The popularity of the grapefruit diet brought the pink grapefruit on to the market in Britain. Until the early 1970s there were times of the year when grapefruit was not available. So great was the demand by hopeful slimmers that one retail marketing chain imported the new pink variety to fill the seasonal gap. Although the grapefruit diet has joined all the other failures, the pink grapefruit remains as an addition to our range of available fruits.

TEA

It was the afternoon tea break which was credited with the might of the old British Empire. If tea were not so common a drink it could well be promoted as having special medicinal properties. Apart from its vast range of chemical substances, including of course the well-known drug caffeine, according to the *Chinese Materia Medica* 'it clears the voice, gives brilliance to the eye, invigorates the constitution, improves the mental faculties, opens up the avenues of the body (!) and regulates the body temperature.' One variety even dissolves metals like gold and iron.

Should this quotation seem to be unacceptable old-fashioned hyperbole, it is as well to remember that ordinary tea was sold in Great Britain in 1983 (until stopped by the Trading Standards Officer) as a slimming agent – 'you lose weight with every sip' – and many people bought it. The ban on that particular product did not stop other people selling tea for slimming until they, too, were stopped.

LIPOLYSIS

Lipolysis is the chemical word for the hydrolysis of fat (triglyceride) into its constituent fatty acids and glycerine. This happens to a partial extent during digestion; part of the dietary fat is absorbed without prior lipolysis.

The term therefore offers attractions to the slimmers' market. The Pountney Clinic advertised a 'revolutionary' treatment that removes fat by dissolving it (this is not lipolysis anyway) so that it can be drawn off as a liquid. Many fat people would certainly feel that this was worth paying for, but the

ASA upheld a complaint by a member of the public who challenged the veracity of the claim and the safety of the treatment *(Case Report 94, Feb. 1983)*. The advertisers stated that they would provide evidence but gave an assurance that meanwhile the advertisement would not be repeated.

LIQUID PROTEIN

One of the most appalling episodes in slimming history took place in the United States with what was called liquid protein. This was a drink intended as a meal replacement. It provided all the nutrients needed, but no calories, and was made from beef hide – which is protein – treated with acid (hydrolysed) to turn it into liquid. The inventor, an osteopath called Dr. Robert Linn, described his preparation in his book as being made from beef hides but told Dr. T. Berland (according to *Rating the Diets, Consumer Guide, 1983 edition)* that it also contained liquid protein derived from sow underbelly. Similar products sprang up all over America and were sold over the counter in shops and drug stores.

Liquid protein became so popular that by the mid-70s millions of Americans were buying it, but as many as 60 had died.

In 1978 the U.S. Centre for Disease Control described the cause of death from prolonged dieting on these products as 'sudden death or death due to intractable cardiac arrythmias in individuals with no previous history of heart disease'. Dr. Linn's original product was intended to be taken only under medical supervision, but since it was on general sale anyone could – and did – buy it, particularly as it was described in a paperback book available to the public.

The utter irresponsibility of the health food movement is illustrated by the fact that although the American deaths had taken place over several years and the official statement quoted above was published in 1978, a free news sheet *Health Now, Issue No. 6, Spring 1979* carried an article by Sheila Graham – who would be expected to be aware of the American experience – recommending liquid protein. Ms. Graham stated, 'I have selected just one (of the 'natural' slimming products) and this new one seems to be catching on in a big way. The idea behind it came from America last year.' At the time of writing, it has been around for some ten years and had already been banned in the United States.

The article went on to describe the way in which the protein powder should be mixed with water and taken instead of food. It added that the manufacturers, Bilson's, say they do not recommend more than three days at a time without consulting a doctor because 'it is a drastic way to tackle a slimming problem'. Since it killed so many people it certainly was drastic. It is of no use advising customers not to continue for more than three days at a time because once such a product is on the market it is certain that some people will take it for much longer than advised.

After describing two slimming preparations – cider vinegar/lecithin/kelp/vitamin B6 and a pre-digested protein from America (subsequently banned there) Sheila Graham went on to say: 'These are just two items in the health food stores, one very well established (that is cider vinegar, lecithin etc.) and the other new (that is the ten year old liquid protein), you won't find these products in the supermarkets or Boots.' The news-sheet containing this article was given away in health food shops and indicates the serious irresponsibility of such shops.

8

WHAT IS
A HEALTHY DIET?

There is no such thing as a perfect diet, but vast numbers of good diets. While we in the Western world eat bread, potatoes, meat and dairy foods, there are people in other parts of the world who live mainly on diets of maize and peanuts, sorghum and fish or even rice and caterpillars, together with a variety of fruit, vegetables and small amounts of other foods. As long as they get enough to eat, all these people can be equally well nourished on their different diets.

Caterpillars, dogs or horsemeat may not sound attractive to us, particularly in Great Britain, but the last is well received in France, along with snails and frogs' legs. Sour pickled cabbage, sauerkraut, is much more common in Germany than England, and pasta is more common in Italy. Olives and olive oil are important parts of the diet in many Mediterranean countries while dates, an occasional fruit in England and the United States, are a major food in some of the Arab countries.

If the Englishman shudders at the thought of monkeys' brains or pigs' fallopian tubes, what would he think of the practice of mixing the ovum of one species of animal with the secretion of the mammary gland of another and frying them together – sometimes called an omelette?

The French eat about ten times as much cheese as the British and drink about twenty times as much wine; the Argentinians eat far more meat than anyone else and half of India is rice-eating while the other half is wheat-eating. In

Ethiopia the main cereal food is teff, quite unknown in Europe. In Nepal the radishes grow a foot long.

Each, then, according to his own tastes and traditions. Most of us eat the kind of food that we are used to, and are often conservative in our habits. While new foods do sometimes gain popularity, our basic foods are the same as our grandparents ate.

WHAT IS A GOOD DIET?

In its simplest terms, a good diet is eating a little of everything and not too much of anything.

We need to eat a little of everything because no food contains all the nutrients – vitamins, mineral salts, certain types of fats and the twenty amino acids. We can get all these different nutrients only if we eat a variety of foods – cereals, vegetables, fruit, dairy produce, fish, meat, chicken, beans and peas. We don't have to eat any one of these – no food is essential – as is proved by those healthy vegans who do not eat any animal food at all. But the greater the variety of food eaten, the greater the chance of getting all the nutrients in adequate amounts.

Nor should we eat too much of anything because some nutrients, as I have explained, are toxic in large amounts. Moreover, we are eating more fat and probably more sugar than is good for us, hence the second half of the nutritional advice, 'not too much of anything'.

WHAT THE NUTRIENTS ARE FOR

All food, whether fish and chips, beans on toast, meat with vegetables or even trifles and desserts, consists of three major nutrients, proteins, fat and carbohydrates, a large group of minor nutrients, the vitamins, another group of minor nutrients, the mineral salts and the attractive chemicals by the thousands that give our food its flavour and colour. The body needs all of these nutrients for growth, repair of tissues and the ordinary daily activities of work and play.

PROTEINS

Flesh and blood consist largely of protein, as do the organs of the body, i.e. the heart, kidney and liver. We cannot make protein so we must eat it. Fortunately, just as human tissues are made from protein, all other living things contain protein.

It is obvious that if human flesh is protein then animal flesh – meat, poultry and fish – are also made from protein and can provide us with the protein we need. It is not so obvious that the cereals – wheat, rice, barley, maize and all the others – also contain protein. In fact, most of the protein in the diets of human beings across the world comes from cereals because those are the main foods eaten. Even in Great Britain, where there is plenty of meat, cheese, fish and milk, we still get one quarter of our protein from cereals.

Foods differ in the amount of protein they contain. Potatoes are often thought of as starch and indeed they do contain 20 per cent starch, but they also contain 1.4 per cent protein. This is not much compared with the 20 per cent in meat, but we eat so many potatoes in Britain that we get more protein from potatoes (3.5 per cent of the average diet) than from eggs (3.2 per cent of the average diet). Fish is a rich source but we eat so little that we only get some 4.5 per cent that way – again, little more than from our potato consumption.

Boiled cabbage may be 90 per cent water, but it also contains 1.3 per cent protein; stewed rhubarb is 95 per cent water but supplies 0.6 per cent protein. We get more than 10 per cent of our protein from fruit and vegetables.

It is only when ingredients are separated that we find foodstuffs that are only starch or fat without any protein. Olives and maize grain contain protein but when oil is pressed from the olive we get fat and when maize is separated we get starch. In their original state all plants, animals, yeasts, bacteria and algae contain protein. Honey is perhaps the only foodstuff that occurs in nature without protein; everything else was a living plant or animal and, as living tissue, contained protein.

PLENTY OF PROTEIN
There is no need to worry about our intake of protein – we all get enough. We eat to satisfy our appetite, which makes sure that we do not go short of fuel (calories). Indeed, as many of us know, our appetites can go too far in that direction so that we can easily eat more calories than necessary and store the surplus against a rainy day that never comes.

Many foods consist largely of carbohydrates, with the result that about half the total calories of the Western diet are in the form of starch and sugar. Some 40 per cent comes from fat, leaving 12 per cent of our diet as protein. Since we need only 6 per cent, we automatically get enough if we satisfy our appetite. It would need a very good cook to devise a menu that tasted good but did not contain sufficient protein to satisfy our needs. This point must be stressed as people will try to sell protein-enriched foods and protein and amino acid supplements when we do not need them. Many vegetarians and vegans worry about their protein intake because they are not eating the more concentrated sources such as meat and fish, but they are still getting enough from other foods.

VITAMINS AND MINERALS

It is the micronutrients, present in foods in very small amounts but also needed in only small amounts, that can give rise to problems. We soon know if we are not eating enough food because we feel hungry but it is possible to serve an attractive, tasty meal which does not contain enough of the nutrients essential to life. It is quite possible – albeit unlikely – to eat expensive, attractive foods which would allow you to die from malnutrition. Most people who can afford to eat well usually eat a wide variety of foods and will get the nutrients they need, but extreme cases could occur. A meal starting with caviar or smoked salmon, followed by beef steak, canned bean sprouts and fried mushrooms and finished with cheese, biscuits, trifle and brandy contains no vitamin C. If you lived on this kind of diet for a few months, you would probably die of scurvy.

WHAT THE VITAMINS DO

All vitamins are essential; we cannot make them so must eat them, otherwise life cannot continue.

Over the centuries in countries around the world people have suffered severe illnesses with many thousands of deaths from shortages of certain vitamins – so these are the ones that are of the greatest nutritional importance. There are six of them, all but one with a letter as well as a chemical name: vitamins A (retinol), B1 (thiamin), B2 (riboflavin), niacin (no number), C (ascorbic acid) and D (cholecalciferol).

VITAMIN A

Vitamin A is present in food in two forms: as carotene, which gives the bright orange colour to carrots, and as ready-made retinol known to most of us in cod-liver oil.

Carotene is changed into retinol in the intestines. You can see it in the orange or yellow colour – yellow when there is less and orange when there is more – in fruit such as mangoes, apricots and peaches and of course in carrots. One carrot has enough to keep us going for a week or two. It is also present in green leaves, but the yellow colour is hidden by the green of the chlorophyll.

There is a large amount of ready-made retinol in the livers of all animals as well as the cod fish and the very rich halibut liver oil. It is also present in milk, cream and butter.

It would be difficult, then, to go short of vitamin A in this part of the world, but it is a major nutritional problem in the south-east Pacific area. It is estimated that one million children a year go blind in Asia and that 10 million are affected. There is a double problem. Not enough vitamin A or carotene is eaten and only part of it is absorbed because there isn't enough fat in the diet.

On average in the West we consume about 40 per cent of the energy of our diet as fat; in the Pacific areas this can be as low as 10 per cent, not quite enough to enable their small intake of vitamin A to be completely absorbed.

Vitamin A protects the cells that keep the various tubes in the body – including the respiratory and intestinal tracts – in their normal healthy, moist condition. When the cells lining the tear ducts and the cornea of the eye dry up, the major signs of vitamin A deficiency (xerophthalmia) can result. If vitamin A is given at this stage the damage can be reversed, but if it is allowed to develop, the eye is irretrievably damaged.

The needs of children are proportionately greater than those of adults as vitamin A is also involved in growth, so it is mostly children who suffer from a deficiency.

B VITAMINS

Although there are a number of B vitamins, the three main ones are grouped together because they all play a part in burning up carbohydrates to provide the energy the body requires.

All the starches and sugars we eat are digested to form, eventually, glucose. The glucose is burned up in the body in about twenty stages to provide four Calories from each gram. It eventually becomes carbon dioxide, which we breathe out, and water. Vitamins B1, B2 and niacin are involved at various stages of this combustion process.

VITAMIN B1

A shortage of vitamin B1 (thiamin) leads to beri-beri. Once very common in the Far East, it is still seen in parts of China and Japan today. Historically beri-beri was blamed on polished rice because it was the introduction of milling and polishing brown rice that removed the vitamin and caused the disease. There is nothing wrong with polished rice when it is a small part of the diet but when it comprises most of the diet – 75 per cent – and few other foods supplying the vitamin are eaten, beri-beri follows. This illustrates the advice not too eat too much of anything.

Recently there have been several hundred cases of beri-beri among high school adolescents in modern, rich Japan due to a diet containing very little B1 – white rice, white flour, sugar and fizzy drinks. Even in a rich country it is possible to make a poor choice of diet. Modern food technology has provided us with a great variety of foods so that we should easily be able to eat 'a little of everything' but a vast variety cannot prevent us making poor choices.

NIACIN (NICOTINIC ACID)

A shortage of niacin leads to pellagra which was extremely common throughout Europe in the eighteenth and nineteenth centuries. It was still a major cause of death in the southern parts of the United States as recently as the 1930s. The real problem was that people lived largely on maize which is a poor source of niacin.

Pellagra is not a problem today in the industrialized countries because niacin is present in all cereals, other than maize, especially whole grain cereals or wholemeal bread. It is added to white bread in many countries and is present in small amounts in many vegetables, tea and coffee. But it still causes problems in parts of India and Africa.

VITAMIN B2

No name has been given as yet to the deficiency disease caused by a lack of vitamin B2, or riboflavin. When it is in short supply the lips and corners of the mouth develop cracks and the tongue and mouth become very painful. It is one of the commonest diseases in the world as few foods contain reasonably large amounts of B2. The only two rich sources are milk and liver, and there is a small amount in cereals and vegetables so we never see the problem in Western countries. In developing countries liver and milk are rarely available so the disease is widespread.

VITAMIN C

A deficiency of vitamin C leads to scurvy. This, as explained earlier, was prevalent among sailors and has a long history.

Before the days of freezing, canning and controlled drying, there was no way to keep fruit and vegetables – the only source of vitamin C – in an edible condition for long sea voyages.

Vitamin C maintains the cementing substances between the cells of our tissues in a normal condition – rather like regularly repointing the cement between bricks. When it is in short supply the cement breaks down and blood leaks through the walls of the smaller blood vessels. Such is scurvy. Fruit and vegetables vary enormously in the amount of vitamin C they contain. Oranges, lemons and grapefruit are rich sources and blackcurrants are extremely rich. Some vegetables, such as lettuce, cucumber and radishes, are very poor sources. Apples do not have very much but the berries and soft fruits are rich enough to provide adequate amounts even after they have been bottled or canned.

VITAMIN D

A shortage of vitamin D leads to rickets, a disease so common in Northern Europe in the seventeenth, eighteenth and nineteenth centuries that it was called, rather unfairly, the English disease.

It is most unusual as a nutrient because it can actually be made in the skin through the effect of sunshine so we do not have to take it in food. We normally get it both ways but it does pose a problem among elderly people who are housebound and do not get much sunshine or do not eat the few foods that contain vitamin D. These are limited to oily fish such as herrings, sardines and pilchards, butter and margarine (to which it is added during manufacture) and a little in eggs. Very few other foods contain enough to be worth mentioning.

We need vitamin D to help our bodies to absorb calcium from our food and also to deposit it on the bones. Children who do not get enough vitamin D have soft bones that bend when the child starts to walk, leading to knock-knees or bow-legs. Between the First and Second World Wars this was a common sight in the slum areas of all British cities. It has largely disappeared now, at least in such a severe form, because we have cleaner air that allows more sunlight to reach us and vitamin D is added to margarine and most baby foods.

Although adults' bones are fully formed, our bodies are always in a state of change. Some calcium is being taken off the bones and fresh calcium laid down to keep us in a good state of repair. When there is a shortage of vitamin D no fresh calcium is deposited leading to the adult equivalent of rickets, which is osteomalacia.

The other vitamins play their essential rôles in the body but rarely present nutritional problems. Vitamin B6 is concerned with the metabolism of amino acids; B12 and folic acid are concerned with blood formation; E is concerned with protecting the fat in our cells from oxidizing; H is necessary for the metabolism of glucose and fats; K is essential for blood clotting; pantothenic acid links together carbohydrate and fat metabolism.

None of these presents a nutritional problem because they are found in so many foods that we all get enough. For example, the name pantothenic acid comes from the Greek 'everywhere' because it is so widely distributed in foods.

There are three other substances that may or may not be essential to human beings and so are not yet definitely known to be vitamins: choline, inositol and PABA (para-amino benzoic acid). Obviously if there is a doubt they cannot be a problem.

MINERAL SALTS
There are at least twenty-one mineral salts essential for the proper functioning of the body. They are needed in very different amounts, for example calcium and phosphate are the main ingredients of bones and are needed in amounts reaching several hundred milligrams daily. Others, such as magnesium, manganese, zinc, copper and chromium function as part of certain enzyme systems and only a few milligrams are needed. Iron is part of the red blood cells and although only about one milligram is needed daily, it is poorly absorbed from food and we must eat at least ten times as much as this.

Most foods contain small amounts of several minerals and a

few foods are particularly good sources. Calcium is present in such large amounts in milk that one pint provides as much as we need in a day. Since it is present in milk, it is also present in cheese and yoghurt, and there are small amounts in many other foods.

Meat is one of the better sources of iron, not only in quantity but because the iron in meat is better absorbed than that of plant foods. This does not make meat an essential food because there are plenty of vegetable sources such as cereals, especially whole grain, wheat germ, wheat bran, soya beans and most vegetables, especially the dark green ones. Among the richest sources of iron are liver and cockles – in fact, all shellfish are rich in iron. Since mild anaemia is fairly common among women the importance of iron in the diet must be stressed.

Lack of iodine causes goitre in some parts of the world. In limestone areas the soil water contains very little iodine, consequently plants growing there contain very little. Where goitre is a problem it is always localized. In England it was found in Derbyshire (and called Derbyshire neck) and to a lesser extent in Oxfordshire because the soil water in those counties was low in iodine. It was found in parts of Switzerland and the United States and is still common, and very severe, in many parts of Africa and Nepal. The problem has disappeared from industrialized countries largely because food is imported from so many other places that the local soil is no longer important in that sense.

The other minerals do not present general nutritional problems because they are provided in so many different foods.

NOT TOO MUCH OF ANYTHING
Some nutrients – especially vitamins D and A but also many other vitamins and some mineral salts – are poisonous and even lethal when taken in excess. Such an excess is rarely possible from food and is usually associated with taking large doses of dietary supplements.

Apart from the toxicity of excess of certain nutrients it is now fairly generally established that many of us take too much fat, sugar and salt for our own good. So the nutritional advice not to eat too much of anything includes these.

DISEASES OF AFFLUENCE

While we have virtually abolished nutritional deficiency diseases in Western countries, we have replaced them with a new set of diseases including coronary heart disease, various disorders of the bowel, certain forms of cancer, high blood pressure, diabetes and several others. They are called diseases of affluence because they seem to occur largely in wealthy, affluent, industrialized countries rather than the poorer developing countries. There is evidence that our diet is partly to blame.

It is difficult to prove this theory because diet is only one of several factors involved in the disorders. For example, in coronary heart disease, which is the principal cause of death in many countries and has arisen only during the last couple of generations, we know that heredity plays perhaps the most important part, that men are affected more than women and that the disease develops with age. In addition to these unchangeable factors, we also know that smoking increases the risk of a heart attack as does obesity and diabetes. An overweight diabetic who smokes heavily has greatly increased chances of dying from coronary heart disease.

Diet is another factor, difficult to prove because it is one of so many, but one that we can do something about. Most scientific authorities believe that fat is the main problem and that we eat too much of it. Saturated fats, the type found mostly in animal foods, increase the amount of cholesterol in the blood and this is known to increase the risk of heart disease.

Cholesterol in the diet seems to be much less important in affecting the amount in the blood. Many authorities in various countries advise reducing the cholesterol consumed down to about 300 mg a day; the British Committee that published its Report in 1984 stated that the average British intake of

350–450 mg a day is not excessive and has a doubtful effect on blood levels.

If you want to play safe, it is worth knowing that the main sources of cholesterol are eggs, liver and meat. Four to seven eggs each week is a reasonable amount and it is suggested that some of our meat could well be replaced by poultry – which not only has less fat but the fat is less saturated – and fish. Oily fish contain polyunsaturated fats which, as mentioned below, may be beneficial in overcoming some of the effects of saturated fats.

The agreed advice, then, is to eat less fat. Just how much less is difficult or even impossible for the individual to know. The average intake is about 100 g a day and it is suggested that this should be reduced to about 85 g. Since no one knows just how much fat he or she is eating, the only possible course of action is to reduce our fat consumption as much as we can. This is not an easy task because so many of our foods contain fat. Apart from butter, margarine, cooking fat and salad oils, we eat cakes, biscuits, chocolate, cheese, meat, sausages and many other foods containing fat. Eliminating these from our diet would be unpleasant and would severely restrict our intake of nutrients. It is not necessary to eliminate all fat, just to reduce the total amount. We can do this by spreading less fat on bread, drinking milk that is partly (2 per cent fat instead of the usual 4 per cent) or completely skimmed, eating low-fat cheese, less meat and more fish and poultry and removing surplus fat from meat. We can also use less fat in cooking.

While these changes cannot guarantee better health for any individual, they are likely to reduce the risk of heart disease in the country as a whole. It cannot do any harm and it may do a great deal of good.

There is less general agreement about adding poly-unsaturates to our diet. Vegetable oils (with the exception of coconut and olive oil) contain polyunsaturates. Substituting polyunsaturates would help reduce the amount of cholesterol in the blood, but adding it to the diet would increase the total amount of fat. The best solution is to reduce the total intake of fat, and replace some saturated fat with polyunsaturates. We can achieve this by using special margarines and vegetable oils in cooking and by manufacturing food with these oils partly replacing, where possible, the saturated fats.

SALT AND HIGH BLOOD PRESSURE

Another food that we take in large amounts is salt. We only need 2 g daily, half of which is the important part, sodium. On average we eat 6 g of sodium, 12 g of salt, each day and some people take a great deal more, sprinkling it over food before they have even tasted it.

High blood pressure is a common disorder in industrialized countries and a contributory factor in many other illnesses. There is some evidence that about 15 per cent of the population is born with the inherited ability to increase blood pressure later in life if they have an excessive salt intake. These people would clearly benefit from a reduced intake throughout their lifetime but they cannot be identified until it is too late. If we all take less salt, therefore, some of us will benefit. It cannot do any harm to reduce the quantity we consume and it might do some people a great deal of good.

DIETARY FIBRE

Everyone nowadays has heard of dietary fibre – a new name for what used to be called roughage. One disease of affluence is diverticular disease of the bowel, common in most industrialized nations and rare in the poor developing countries. There people eat more than 100 g of dietary fibre a day, compared with our 20 g. So it is likely that we might be developing diverticular disease – and several associated disorders including constipation – because we do not eat enough fibre.

The best form of dietary fibre to prevent constipation is cereal bran. Wholemeal bread contains 9 g in 100 g, the equivalent of three slices. White bread contains 4 g. Fruit and vegetables also contain fibre; in fruit it is pectin, in vegetables it is cellulose. The recommendation, then, is to eat more cereals (and that these should be whole grain rather than milled) and more fruit and vegetables.

We should also eat less sugar since it does not provide any nutrients, but only calories, and has been implicated in many disorders ranging from dental decay through obesity to heart disease. Not everyone agrees that sugar is harmful, but everyone does agree that we would benefit from eating less of it. At the very best we could replace sugar with other foods that supply proteins, vitamins and minerals instead of empty calories.

Fat and sugar are best replaced with starchy foods such as bread and potatoes, particularly wholemeal bread and potatoes with their skins on.

The dietary goals can thus be summarized as:

1 If you are overweight, slim down.
2 Eat less fat, particularly the saturated fats.
3 Eat less sugar.
4 Eat more fruit, vegetables, bread and potatoes.
5 Eat cereals as whole grain bread or at least as brown bread and leave potatoes in their skins.
6 Take less salt.

These goals have been recommended in many countries, some of which claim that they are already seeing some degree of success. Deaths from heart disease have been falling for the past few years in the United States and while it is by no means certain that this is due to a change in diet, jogging (exercise does help!), reduced smoking or a combination of the three, the fall is claimed a success for a more sensible life style. The results of a public health campaign have been more dramatic in Norway.

Not even the most optimistic nutritionist expects changes to occur overnight. Some groups have set a target of fifteen years, that is, to improve our diet in the ways suggested by the year 2000. While following the advice may not do any good, it certainly cannot do any harm.

FOOD AND DIET

One last word on this subject is necessary to distinguish between food and diet. People often ask whether certain foods are good or bad. The answer is that there are no bad foods, only bad diets. A little of everything means that you really can eat a chocolate éclair – or half of one if you are trying to lose weight – and you do not have to give up any food completely, not even sugar. What you must do is learn to control the amount eaten. There is no harm in drinking alcohol in moderate amounts (that is, a daily average of not more than two pints of beer, one third of a bottle of wine or three fluid ounces of spirit). In fact, small amounts of alcohol may be actually beneficial in heart disease.

Alcohol and salt serve as examples of moderation. A small amount of salt is essential, just as a vitamin, but a large amount can be lethal. The body needs 2 g to function but 10 g may raise the blood pressure in some people and 100 g will kill you. So moderation is again the rule.

In the case of alcohol, a moderate amount cannot do any harm, and may be of some benefit, but a large amount can damage the liver and brain.

Moderation is the watchword for all dietary changes. Slimming by starvation is looking for trouble – several deaths have resulted from this kind of severe dieting. We can lose weight at a 'healthy' rate by reducing the food intake level to 1000–1200 Calories daily.

While the food industry has been blamed for putting too much fat, salt and sugar into processed foods, it has also made available foods which allow us to follow the dietary guidelines without too much effort. We can not only buy sugar and salt substitutes, but low-fat preparations and even white bread with enough bran added to give it more fibre than wholemeal bread. So it is possible to follow the dietary guidelines without greatly changing our food habits.

BIBLIOGRAPHY

Balfour, Michael and Allen, Judy, editors *The A to Z of Health Food Terms*, Garnstone Press 1973.

Barker, B. M. and Bender, D. A. *Vitamins in Medicine*, Fourth Edition, Volumes I and II, William Heinemann Medical Books Ltd. 1982.

Bender, A. E. *Whatever Happened to Vitamin B16?* in Chemistry and Industry 1981, Society of Chemical Industry.

Berland, Theodore *Rating the Diets*, Consumer Guide, Publications International Ltd. 1983.

Bircher, Ruth *Eating Your Way to Health*, Faber & Faber 1961. Translated and edited by Claire Loewenfeld.

Blix, Gunnar *Food Cultism and Nutrition Quackery*, Almqvist & Wiksells 1970.

Cowell, Freda M., Cooper, Caroline and Smedley, Gillian M. (Good Housekeeping Institute) *A Comparison of the Taste of 'Organically' Grown Produce with that of Artificially Fertilized Produce*, in Nutrition 1960.

Grant, Doris *Your Daily Bread*, Faber & Faber Ltd. 1944.

Hewitt, James *Kelp – a Cornucopia of Health* in Here's Health, No. 169, September 1970.

Hughes, R. Elwyn *Vitamin C – Some Current Problems*, British Nutrition Foundation 1981.

Mazel, Judy *The Beverly Hills Diet*, Sidgwick & Jackson 1981.

Polunin, Miriam *The Right Way to Eat*, J. M. Dent & Sons 1978.

Stuart, G. A. *Chinese Materia Medica*, Vegetable Kingdom,

Shanghai 1911 (extensively revised from Dr. F. Porter Smith's work).

Waller, Robert, editor *Just Consequences,* Charles Knight 1971.

Watson, Gail C. and Blate, Michael *Cooking Naturally for Pleasure and Health,* Routledge & Kegan Paul 1983.

Watt, Bernice K. and Merrill, Annabel L. *Composition of Foods Agriculture Handbook No. 8,* U.S. Department of Agriculture, U.S. Government Printing Office 1975.

Wheatley, Michael *A Way of Living as a Means of Survival – An Encyclopaedia of Natural Health,* Corgi Books 1977.

Williams R. J. and Kalita, D. K., editors *A Physician's Handbook on Orthomolecular Medicine,* Pergamon Press 1977.

NEWS-SHEETS

Health Now, Digipark Ltd., Surbiton, Surrey.

Healthy Life News, published in Australia.

Holland & Barrett Express, bi-monthly free handout.

Rutin and the Buckwheat Connection Leaflet from Rutin Products, Ltd., Camberley, Surrey – reprinted from an article in Health Now, Autumn 1977.

When – Alternative Medicine, World Health and Ecology News, Roberts Publications. Vol. 1, No. 3, p. 11.

INDEX

Trim those inches!

SUNDAY EXPRESS DIET BOOK

MARINA ANDREW'S

60 TRIED AND TESTED DIETS FOR EVERY OCCASION

For nearly 23 years, readers of the *Sunday Express* have been turning to Marina Andrews' column for helpful advice and, above all, interesting new diets.

Now Marina has gathered the best of them together to give a diet for every lifestyle, a solution for every problem and a flash of inspiration to the all too dull business of dieting.

0 7221 1301 3   HEALTH AND FITNESS   £2.50

LEARN HOW TO OVERCOME TENSION
AND STRESS IN ONLY 30 MINUTES A DAY!

The 10 day Relaxation Plan

DR ERIC TRIMMER

Stress is one of today's biggest killers. The pressures of modern living ensure that most of us at some time will suffer from anxiety and tension, becoming potential victims of stress-related disease. Dr Eric Trimmer explains how we can recognise the first symptoms of stress in our bodies, together with the factors which trigger them – and train ourselves to relax, without recourse to pills or alcohol.

* This is the first book to draw together a variety of disciplines, including yoga and autogenics, to produce a unique plan of simple exercises.
* The exercises are clearly illustrated and arranged in three programmes to suit all ages and levels of fitness.
* Just select the programme which suits you best – whether you're a housewife, pensioner or businessman – and in 10 days learn how to overcome tension and enjoy a healthy body and mind!

HEALTH AND FITNESS   0 7221 8605 3   £1.95

KITTY CAMPION'S

HANDBOOK OF
HERBAL HEALTH

The natural way to a healthier life

Herbalism is the most natural way to get healthy and stay
healthy. This detailed handbook written by a medical
herbalist, tells you everything you need to know about
herbs: how to identify them, collect them, cook with
them and how to prepare traditional herbal remedies for
headaches, high blood pressure, toothache, sunburn and
many other common ailments. There's also advice on
how to make refreshing herbal drinks and details of a
complete herbal cleansing programme that will revitalise
your body.

Covering hundreds of herbs and cures, KITTY
CAMPION'S HANDBOOK OF HERBAL HEALTH
will show you that herbal remedies are as effective today
as they've always been. When you realise the natural
alternatives, you may never have to take an aspirin again.

HEALTH AND MEDICINE   0 7221 2352 3   £2.95

A SELECTION OF BESTSELLERS FROM SPHERE

FICTION

DUNN'S CONUNDRUM	Stan Lee	£2.95 ☐
GOLDEN TALLY	Pamela Oldfield	£2.95 ☐
HUSBANDS AND LOVERS	Ruth Harris	£2.95 ☐
SWITCH	William Bayer	£2.25 ☐

FILM & TV TIE-IN

BOON	Anthony Masters	£2.50 ☐
LADY JANE	Anthony Smith	£1.95 ☐

NON-FICTION

THE FALL OF SAIGON	David Butler	£3.95 ☐
THE AMBRIDGE YEARS	Dan Archer	£2.50 ☐
THE SUNDAY EXPRESS DIET BOOK	Marina Andrews	£2.50 ☐
THE PRICE OF TRUTH	John Lawrenson and Lionel Barber	£3.50 ☐

All Sphere books are available at your local bookshop or newsagent, or can be ordered direct from the publisher. Just tick the titles you want and fill in the form below.

Name _____

Address _____

_____

Write to Sphere Books, Cash Sales Department, P.O. Box 11, Falmouth, Cornwall TR10 9EN

Please enclose a cheque or postal order to the value of the cover price plus:

UK: 45p for the first book, 20p for the second book and 14p for each additional book ordered to a maximum charge of £1.63.

OVERSEAS: 75p for the first book plus 21p per copy for each additional book.

BFPO & EIRE: 45p for the first book, 20p for the second book plus 14p per copy for the next 7 books, thereafter 8p per book.

Sphere Books reserve the right to show new retail prices on covers which may differ from those previously advertised in the text or elsewhere, and to increase postal rates in accordance with the PO.